WING

WALKING

WING
WALKNG

a novel by
HARRY GROOME

THE
CONNELLY
PRESS

For information about special discounts for bulk purchases, please contact
The Connelly Press, PO Box 7341,
Saint Davids, PA 19087.

Book design by Mojo Marketing
Printed and bound by Thomson-Shore, Inc., Dexter, Michigan

Library of Congress Control Number 2007904366
ISBN 978-0-9797415-0-0
1 3 5 7 9 8 6 4 2
FIRST EDITION

A number of the characters' names in this book were drawn from real life to represent the many people I worked with over the years who kept our enterprises headed in the right direction, in the right fashion. *Wing Walking* is dedicated to them with great affection and gratitude.

FOREWORD

The story that follows is a true business story—not a story about balance sheets or supply chains or high finance—but a story of egos and ambition, power and betrayal, and love. The stage was set at the opening reception of the Pharmaceutical Manufacturers Association annual meeting in March of 1989 when a tall, balding man dressed in a double-breasted blue blazer and gray slacks stepped on the diving board that protruded over a lighted swimming pool and tried desperately to be heard above the festive crowd of conventioneers. "Ladies and gentlemen, may I have your attention?" he called out, his English accent lost in the din. "Ladies and gentlemen, if you would, please." The man tapped the highball glass he was holding with a silver pen and raised his voice. "Please. May I have your attention for just a moment?" He surveyed the hundreds of people milling under the terra cotta-tiled archways and about the colorfully lighted fountains of the outdoor reception area of the Boca Raton Resort and Club, and tapped his glass again. "Ladies and gentlemen, if you wouldn't mind, I have a story that I think will amuse you."

A heavyset woman with tightly curled brown hair stepped toward the diving board and looked up at the man through oval horn-rimmed glasses. "Are you sure you're doing the right thing?" she said. "Remember the old axiom, Richard: you only get one chance to make a first impression."

The man glanced down and scowled at his wife. "I have everything under control, Naomi. This isn't about your cherished public relations; it's about one-upmanship. Nothing more."

The spirited murmur of the conventioneers continued as they went on sipping their gin- or rum-and-tonics and white wines and greeting other members of their industry's elite— the top executives from Merck Sharp & Dohme, Pfizer, International Pharmaceutical Products, Eli Lilly, Bristol-Myers, and all the rest. "Quiet!" the man yelled and slowly the chattering eased and many turned their attention to him. "Please," he added with a forced smile, and then said, "Thank you." He slipped his pen inside his blazer and smoothed his narrow gray tie with a long-fingered hand. "As Elizabeth Taylor is rumored to have said to each of her husbands on their wedding night, 'I'll only keep you for a moment.'" There was a ripple of laughter from those closest to him and someone in the back of the crowd yelled, "Louder!"

The man on the diving board raised an index finger and acknowledged the request with a curt salute. "With your permission, I would very much like to tell you a story I heard today." He paused and searched the crowd of blue and lime-green blazers; of glittering jewelry, silk print cocktail dresses and sharply creased silk pants, until he found the men he was looking for, Arch Dolan and his son David, their heads showing above most of the others, one bristling white, the other black and shiny as licorice in the fading twilight. He noted that

the Dolans were with their wives and another company executive and smiled. "For those of you whom I haven't met," he
said, pointing to the name badge clipped to the breast pocket
of his blazer, "I'm Dr. Richard Beecroft, and I've recently
moved to America to take charge of Whitecliff Laboratories'
North American operations."

Arch Dolan laid a thick-knuckled hand on his son's shoulder and asked, "David, what's this shifty bastard up to now?"

"I have no idea," David answered. "But, don't worry, Dad,
if it's about us, it won't help him in court."

Bud Haney, the Sales Vice President for Dolan Laboratories, turned toward his colleagues, his short-cropped red hair
and ruddy complexion glowing scarlet in the flickering light of
the hurricane lanterns that lit the reception; his strong, pro-
nounced jaw set as if he expected a fight; the hint of a smile
and the brightness of his hazel eyes making him look as
though he was enjoying the moment. He looked at the older
Dolan and said in a thick Alabama drawl, "Even money says
you're not going to like what old Richard's up to, court or no
court, lawsuit or no lawsuit."

Richard swept his hand that held his half-empty glass above
the crowd to signal that he was addressing each and every one.
"I find this story so timely and so appropriate. It's the story of a
wealthy Arab sheik who has just learned that he is dying of cancer and wants to make one last loving gesture to each of his
three sons." He smiled briefly, looked from left to right, and
then settled his close-set dark eyes on the Dolan contingent.

As Richard fixed his gaze once again on her family, Elizabeth Dolan raised her slight frame on the balls of her feet and
shifted from one foot to the other in an effort to see around
the conventioneers in front of her. Finally, she gave up and
leaned toward her husband and whispered, "Please, Arch,
don't be too upset. He's only telling a joke."

Arch raised his bushy white eyebrows and looked down at Elizabeth as she slipped her hand into his large, powerful grasp. "Who the hell does he think he is, anyway? This is unheard of."

"I know." Elizabeth gently squeezed his hand. "But still, dear, try not to get upset."

While Elizabeth tried to comfort her husband, Bud gathered David and his wife close to him by wrapping his powerful arms around their shoulders. He glanced first at Susan and then at David. "This could get interesting."

David patted him on the small of his back and smiled. Bud and he had worked together for fifteen years and had become fast friends, both at work and at play, and Susan and their three daughters had accepted him as a member of their family. The challenge of the lawsuit with Richard Beecroft had brought these men even closer together to battle a common enemy, an enemy who in response to the Dolans' charges of restraint of trade, had questioned their integrity.

Richard continued. "So from his deathbed the sheik offered each of his sons one last wish. The older boy asked for a new car, and his father honored his request and gave him a whole fleet of cars: Bentleys, Rolls Royces, Jaguars, the whole lot. The middle son wanted a new boat and the sheik again honored this request and gave his son his own personal navy, one that included sailboats, speedboats, and boats for offshore fishing."

Richard found himself addressing a now quiet—perhaps curious—audience and a smile spread across his face and his dark eyes brightened. He took a sip from his glass and leaned his gangling frame slightly forward in the direction he was looking, forward toward the Dolans who, along with Bud Haney, had knotted together as though they were circling their family wagons. "The youngest son, who was still just a small boy, said that all he wanted was for his father to get well and that he needed a new pair of Mickey Mouse pajamas. And so the sheik thanked

4

his son for his caring and bought him a new Mickey Mouse outfit." Richard stared hard at Arch and David to make sure they were looking at him. When their eyes met his, he raised his hands above his head as though he had just won a footrace and bellowed, "And buy him a Mickey Mouse outfit he did. He bought him Dolan Laboratories!"

There were a few faint laughs and then an uncomfortable silence.

Arch took David by his arm and grabbed Bud by the back of his jacket as he began to push through the crowd toward Richard. "No!" Arch said. "We'll have none of that."

Bud turned and looked at Arch. "Yes, sir, Mr. Dolan, but just once—just once—I'd like to wipe that smug—"

"I understand," Arch said, "but we're leaving. Quietly. Like gentlemen. But don't worry boys, I'll fight that son of a bitch to the end. No one humiliates my family in public. No one."

Slowly, as all eyes focused on the family, Arch and Elizabeth edged their way through the crowd, walking deliberately toward the hotel, hand in hand, neither looking left nor right, Elizabeth somehow keeping stride with her husband as though their forty-five years of marriage had prepared them for just such an occasion. Many of the conventioneers lowered their voices or stopped talking altogether as they neared them. Some smiled and uttered small pleasantries; a few patted Arch on the shoulder as he passed.

David swept his right leg in a semicircle as he limped behind his parents. He smiled and nodded good-naturedly to everyone who spoke to his father, as though it was his role as the heir apparent to acknowledge each comment of support, each display of friendship and respect.

Susan followed David and her in-laws, her arms wrapped across her waist with her hands clenching the ends of a turquoise shawl that she had drawn tightly across her shoulders.

Her apricot-blonde hair was pulled back from her face and ran underneath her shawl in a broad braid that reached midway between her shoulder blades. "What was that man thinking?" she muttered. "Didn't he know he'd only make things worse?"

Bud Haney walked a few steps behind the family, his hands jammed deep in his pants pockets. Known by the Dolan employees as the "spare" in the heir and the spare equation of their company's succession plan, he nodded at many of the Dolan well-wishers, saying to one, "That old Richard's one tough dog to keep under the porch."

Across the reception area, Richard stepped from the diving board and worked his way toward the Dolans. His wife followed him—occasionally calling his name and reaching for his hand to stop his slalom through the crowd—but his long strides kept him just out of her reach. When he was no more than twenty feet from the Dolans, a heavily jowled man whose name badge displayed a blue ribbon with *Committee* written on it in gold letters, stepped in front of him. "Dr. Beecroft, enough is enough," the man said. "I think you should end your little joke right here."

From behind him, Naomi said, "Please, Richard, listen to the gentleman. You've done enough damage for one night."

Richard appeared not to hear her and stared at the man, then raised his long right index finger to his eyebrow and saluted. "All in good fun, you know." He stepped around the man and again started toward the Dolans.

"Dr. Beecroft, I said no more," the committee official said. "This meeting's always been a friendly gathering and we don't want that to change now. This type of thing is out of place, out of order."

Richard stopped for a moment and looked back at the committee member. "What do you take me for?" He glared at him. "And who are you anyway?" Before the man could answer,

Richard took several long strides, spun on the ball of one foot and the heel of the other in military fashion, and blocked the Dolans' path.

Arch slowed momentarily and turned to David and then looked over his shoulder at Bud. "Don't give him the satisfaction of a scene. That's not the Dolan way." He smiled at Elizabeth and she looked up and smiled back at him and they began to walk around Richard, their eyes once again fixed straight ahead.

"Mr. Dolan, do you have time for a question?" Richard said.

"I've answered all the questions I'm going to," Arch said. "Your lawyers, with all their goddamn depositions, know all you need to know."

Arch and his family continued to walk, but stopped when Richard asked, "Why don't you settle this frivolous little case?"

Arch blurted out, "Over my dead body!" and then looked at the cluster of men standing behind Richard. Most were friends—a few his colleagues for all or most of the thirty years he'd been Chairman and Chief Executive of Dolan Laboratories. Some, like the family members from GD Searle and AH Robbins, shared his fierce pride in their company's name and reputation, and coveted their family's privacy. "Did you hear that?" Arch said. "*Now* he wants to settle." He laughed and his friends laughed with him, and then he turned his watery blue stare toward Richard. "Settle? After what you've just done?" He shook his head in disgust. "You should have known better, Dr. Beecroft. Now, I'll fight you to the bitter end." He beckoned to David, Susan and Bud. "Enough of this nonsense. Let's go to dinner."

David limped behind his parents with Susan now at his side. As they passed Richard, Richard asked, "David, did you see the humor in my little story?"

"Richard, for Christ's sake, leave well enough alone,"

David said. "This is neither the time nor the place for this." He looked at Richard with pale blue eyes identical to his father's and lowered his voice. "If there's something you want to discuss, call me. But for now, just drop it."

Richard stepped aside and watched the Dolans walk away. "It's true, you know," he called to them.

The Dolans kept walking but Haney stopped. "What's true?"

"Come on, Bud, let's go," David said over his shoulder. "He's just trying to bait us."

"Right," Bud said, "and this country boy's taking the bait."

Arch stopped abruptly. "Bud, I said there'd be none of that. We'll handle this like gentleman, even if Dr. Beecroft won't."

"Yes, sir," Bud said, "but I'm still a bit curious to know what he thinks is true."

The committee member from the PMA told Richard to rejoin the reception, that his joke had gone far enough, but Richard simply dismissed him with a wave of his hand and said to Bud, "If you weren't so enamored of the Dolan family, you'd know what's true. You'd know you're working for a Mickey Mouse outfit."

Bud looked to Arch. "You have my word for it, sir, I won't cause any trouble; I'd just like a brief word with old Dr. Mickey Mouse." He took a step toward Richard and as Richard took a step back, and then another, the crowd behind him moved as well. Before Richard could step back again, Bud grabbed him by the biceps of his left sleeve, and pulled him close. Richard tried to free his arm but Bud held fast, his thick, freckled hand white at its knuckles. "Richard," he whispered, "these people are like family to me and you're trying to make fools of them. Well, mark my words, if you ever try anything like this again—ever again—I'll break your fucking neck." He jerked Richard closer and then let go of him.

Richard stared down at him and massaged his arm. "So the Dolans' minion has spoken, has he? Well, we'll see who comes out on top at the end of the day."

"I can't wait," Bud said, and rejoined the Dolans as they hurried toward the hotel.

Richard turned and walked back through the crowd to his wife who stood expressionless, her arms folded across her chest. "Are you satisfied?" she asked.

"It's all of more consequence to you and the Dolans than it is to me," he said. "You all are so concerned with image. You must understand, these people are used to this type of brashness. They're Americans."

"Look around you," Naomi said. "Do these people look like they're here to carry out their corporate wars or embarrass one another? Quite the contrary, Richard. And all you've done is embarrass yourself—and me, for that matter—and for no apparent reason other than you wanted to make your presence known. I told you not to tell that story but you wouldn't listen. You never do. Even when I'm supposed to know better." She paused, for Richard was looking over her head at the throng of people behind her and waited for him to look back at her. "Well, Richard, why don't you ever pay any attention? Why did you even bother to bring me here?"

Richard smiled. "It's an important meeting for me and we should be seen together."

"So image is important after all?"

"I don't have time for word games right now," Richard said. "Come, there are several people we should say hello to."

"No. You go," Naomi said. "I'm going to our room. I've had enough of all this—enough of you—for one night."

Ten years later, these executives became entangled once again.

For David Dolan, who was named Chairman and Chief Executive Officer of his family's business when his father relinquished the post, events were set in motion by a phone call from the Food and Drug Administration.

For Richard Beecroft, appointed Chairman and CEO of Whitecliff Laboratories after his return from New York to their headquarters in London, his problems began with pressure from the Prime Minister's office.

And for Bud Haney, who resigned from Dolan Laboratories shortly after David became CEO, and who eventually became Chief Executive of International Pharmaceutical Products, his pivotal role in all of this began with a surprise visit from his old nemesis.

What follows is their story.

CHAPTER 1

David Dolan had taken the call from the FDA at 11:35 a.m. on Friday, August 27. He remembered the moment precisely because he was staring at the large oval clock on the wall opposite his desk as the woman with the whining nasal voice from the Office of Drug Evaluation said, "I'll get right to the point, Dr. Dolan. We've got a very serious situation on our hands. In the past week we've received reports of at least six deaths—and possibly others—due to hepatic failure with patients on Dolatriptan."

David had wanted to correct her, that it was *mister* Dolan, not *doctor,* and that she must have her other facts wrong as well, for his company was aware of isolated reports of minor *kidney* related side effects, not *liver,* and that they had no reports of anyone dying while taking Dolatriptan. But the woman had emphasized "at least six deaths due to *hepatic* failure," and repeated it twice before David heard her say, "I'm afraid, Dr. Dolan, your company must immediately implement a Class I recall."

"Recall Dolatriptan?" His voice faltered as he asked the question, for up until that moment he had thought that Dolatriptan, a drug that was showing every sign of becoming the cornerstone of his family's business for years to come, had an excellent safety profile. And suddenly he realized that his company was in serious trouble, and there was going to be hell to pay in a number of quarters, not the least of which would be with his father.

Now, as he pushed his Porsche ten miles an hour, then twenty, above the speed limit, these thoughts clicked over and over in his mind, the way he remembered the music from his childhood Victrola when its needle couldn't move to the next groove, each click punctuated by *and I've got to tell Dad and recommend the unthinkable*. The thought of his father caused him to draw a deep breath and accelerate until he was cruising at seventy miles per hour, for he didn't want to start off their meeting by being late.

His wife, Susan, seated in the beige leather bucket seat next to him, pushed her purse between her sandaled feet and ordered the flap of her denim skirt across her tanned thighs. "David, slow it down a bit," she said. "The problem's not going anywhere."

He backed off until the speedometer read forty miles per hour. "Maybe for once he'll understand; maybe even give me the benefit of the doubt. Anyway, if it all comes unraveled, I can always change my mind."

"Uh-uh," Susan said. "Once you tell him what you're thinking there won't be any turning back, so you'd better make up your mind, once and for all, if you're really going to go through with this."

For a moment David was silent, trying to get the pieces to settle in place. "But it's the right thing to do." He glanced at Susan. "Hell, it's the only thing to do." He pulled down on the arm of the directional signal and swung the Porsche into the heavily wooded entrance to Fox Hill Farm. He had chosen Fox Hill because he thought his father would best receive the bad news, and feel more open to discuss the future of his family's business in familiar surroundings. He thought that at least he couldn't be faulted for *that* decision, for it was on this two hundred-acre spread of rolling countryside fifteen minutes west of Princeton that his parents had lived for over fifty years, and other than their sons and three grandchildren—and Dolan Laboratories—Fox Hill Farm was all they seemed to live for. But he also knew that the odds that his father would accept his recommendation, no matter where or when he delivered it, were very low.

The sound of the Porsche speeding over a wooden-slat bridge, the bridge rolling out its familiar thunder-like rumble, caused him to brake his car and for an instant he was seventeen again, had just been expelled from Philips Exeter Academy for smoking marijuana and saw the gray form of the deer, its antlers chalk white in the headlight of his motorcycle, its frightened eyes reflecting back at him, saw it flick its large white flag and start to jump across the bridge when his motorcycle hit the animal square in the hindquarters and he was suddenly soaring over the deer, whooping joyously that he could fly, until in the darkness, in his altered state, the effects of marijuana and gin still holding him afloat, he saw where he was about to land, his right hip and thigh crashing down on a rough, whitewashed stone the size of a large pumpkin, one of the many whitewashed stones placed by his father every ten yards along the drive to mark the way to the Fox Hill farmhouse.

When they found him—three boys his same age, out on a joyride jacking deer with a spotlight on their car; boys who had followed the crippled buck as it dragged its hindquarters back down the drive—he was unconscious and they had woken his parents yelling that some guy driving a motorcycle was lying in the driveway out cold and badly hurt, and his mother had run to him dressed only in her nightgown and slippers, and as he gained consciousness heard her screaming, "David, are you all right? Oh, God, please son, be all right," and he remembered his father following her, cinching the sash to his maroon silk bathrobe tight across his waist, bellowing, "What in God's name has he done now?"

And David thought that his father's reaction to their upcoming discussion might be very much the same and imagined him screaming, "What in God's name are you doing now?" He sensed that his recommendation, like so many other things, would be viewed as a failure on his part, and he hoped that his mother could somehow soften the blow. Her words when he phoned to say he'd been thrown out of Exeter still comforted him. "Are you terribly upset?" she had asked, and when he had told her no, she said, "Well, then, your father and I aren't either." But he soon learned that this kind thought was hers alone, that his father was disappointed in him, but more important, embarrassed by him; that the humiliation he had brought upon his father and the Dolan name would color their relationship from then on.

He eased the Porsche from beneath the trees into the open where black-faced sheep grazed quietly in grassy fields bordered by post-and-rail fences; braked in front of the 19th-century fieldstone farmhouse, parking side by side with a black Ford Taurus station wagon, and pulled himself free from his car, easing his thin right thigh beneath the steering wheel and across the seat with the help of his hands. He limped behind the Porsche, running a hand over the low-slung car's metallic-blue roof. As he pulled the door open for Susan, a Border collie, his penetrating eyes fixed on David, ran to greet him. He bent and gently massaged the inside of one of the dog's ears, then straightened and faced his childhood home. To the right of the house, a large American flag flapped slowly at half-mast, as it had every day since March 4, 1968, the day his parents received word that their older son had been killed in Vietnam. He slid his heels together and saluted. *Where are you when I need you most?* When he turned to face Susan, she was smiling. "Nice," she said. "Every time, I think it's nice."

David nodded and took her arm and they walked around the side of house to a small set of ivy-bordered steps that led to a flagstone terrace. He knew he'd find his parents there, and imagined them in their familiar Sunday routine, seated in wrought-iron porch chairs in the shade of an expansive locust tree, facing down the grassy hillside toward the willow-lined pond, *The New York Times* held in place on a glass-top table by an oval stone the size of a softball. He thought his father would be wearing a pair of orthopedic leather shoes and, like him, khaki trousers—his father's a bit baggy in the seat and too short at the cuffs—and a frayed Lacoste polo shirt. He would be drinking iced tea. His mother would have on a cotton wraparound skirt and a print blouse. Her green and tan gardening gloves, and a spade and a trowel would be placed neatly alongside her chair, and by now she would have read the travel section of *The Times* from cover to cover and would have begun to fuss about making lunch.

He stepped aside to let Susan climb the stairs ahead of him. As she passed him, she kissed him lightly on the cheek and whispered, "Stay the course."

Elizabeth Dolan stood as Susan and David reached the top of the steps. She closed the flap of her green skirt against the warm August breeze, slipped off her glasses, leaving them to dangle from a thin gold chain, and welcomed her son and daughter-in-law, taking their hands firmly and beaming as she asked how they were and how her granddaughters were doing.

David wrapped his arms around her narrow shoulders and kissed her on the forehead. "All's well at home," he answered hurriedly. "Where's Dad?"

"He's in the library; says it's too bright out here for him to read." She took his hands and squeezed them again. "He's worried sick about your visit."

Arch Dolan carefully marked the page in the book he was reading as David entered the room and leaned toward him and hugged him around the neck. Arch patted him on the back and said, "You've got bad news for me."

"Well, sir—"

"Come on, David," Arch said, "your mother told me you wanted to talk about a problem at the office, and that's not like you, unless things are pretty bad."

"Right," David said. "How about we take a walk down to the pond? I could use some of your lily pad wisdom."

"Whatever you say," Arch said. He pushed his large frame from the deep chair and steadied himself with a hand on his son's shoulder. "You're the boss."

Once outside, Arch's arthritic hips and David's shortened right leg caused them to shuffle slowly down the grassy hillside toward a large willow that shaded the pond at the foot of the hill. It was here, in this place that was almost sacred to David, that in the summer he and his brother, seated beside their father, caught bass and sunfish and talked about fishing and the wonders of nature. In the winters, he and Arch Jr. skated here every day the ice was thick enough, playing shinny hockey with people of all ages, often with their father as captain of one team and their Uncle Ben captain of the other. As they grew older, the pond-side talks eventually switched to lectures about the essence and importance of their family's business, their "sacred trust." As boys, and then as young men, they were encouraged to assume the responsibilities and obligations that went with their family name and follow their father's familiar refrain: "Family, community, country, and Dolan Laboratories."

In their late teens, Arch Jr. and David's paths parted, although their brotherly bonds never weakened. The fall that David was expelled from Exeter, his brother followed in his grandfather and father's footsteps and entered Princeton. David, on the other hand, missed the remainder of the school year recovering from his accident, graduated from the local country day school a year later and went to Franklin & Marshall College—in his father's words, "a good school, but not in a class with Princeton." It was there, during the second semester of his junior year, that he received a phone call from his father telling him that three Marines had just left Fox Hill and that he'd better come home right away; that his mother needed him home badly.

"Arch has been wounded?" he had said.

"No," his father whispered.

He thought he heard his father swallow. After a moment he said, "It's worse than that isn't it, Dad?" and when his father still didn't speak, he said, "Arch has been killed."

He waited. Finally his father said, "I never thought I'd outlive one of my boys. Please come home, son, right away," and hung up the phone.

With this memory, and aware of the importance of what he was about to recommend, David considered cutting this discussion short and saving his recommendation for another day. His thoughts were interrupted by his father. "It's supposed to reach almost a hundred today. Hottest day on record since the year I was born." He looked directly at him. "Okay, how bad is it?"

David stopped walking and turned his father gently toward him. "We got a call from the FDA on Friday. They've asked us to recall Dolatriptan. We've encountered some very serious side effects."

"I'm sure you can work things through with the FDA," Arch said. "We always have in the past."

"Dad, we've never been in a spot like this before. The FDA's already received reports of six deaths."

Arch raised his bushy white eyebrows, and asked, as though he had something caught in his throat, "Drug-related deaths?"

"Drug-related hepatic failure. The drug's dead, Dad. We've been working on a press release with the FDA and we'll be issuing it first thing tomorrow."

They shuffled a few steps into the shade and watched a frog jump from the tall grass at their feet and kick quickly away beneath a cluster of lily pads into the dark water. Arch rested a closed fist on his son's shoulder. His hand felt comforting to him. "Well, we'll do what we've always done," Arch said. "We'll find another drug. We'll stay the course."

David shook his head and took his father's arm. "Without Dolatriptan our business is going to go to hell in a hand basket and, as promising as it is, lomaxidine won't be ready in time to save us. It's three years from marketing at best." Still holding his father's arm, he took an awkward step to face him. "I think we should sell."

Arch flinched and David felt his arm stiffen. "Sell *what*?"

"Sell the company."

"Never," Arch said, and pulled free from his son.

"But we've explored everything—"

"Licensing a drug from someone else?" Arch said.

"We've tried, but the game's changed. There aren't any that are worth a damn that are available to us."

Arch let out a short laugh and wiped beads of sweat from his forehead with the heel of his hand. "The game couldn't have changed that much."

"It has, Dad. Trust me on this. I've done everything humanly possible to protect our company in case something like this happened. The good news is I get calls all the time asking if we're interested in some kind of deal. There are lots of companies that would love to get their hands on lomaxidine. So, even without Dolatriptan, I'm sure we could get a very good price."

"Who said anything about price?" Arch bellowed. "This isn't about money! This is about our sacred trust; our family's priceless pride."

David lowered his voice, hoping to defuse the conversation. "But, Dad, it's the right business move. Our bankers frequently raise the issue, and so does Uncle Ben."

"To hell with the bankers and to hell with Ben! You're not lining up with him are you?"

"I'm not lining up with anyone," he said. "I'm trying to do what's right for the business and what's best for our family."

Arch waved a hand in front of his chest. "Don't you worry about the family. That's my job. Your job is managing the business." He wiped his brow again. "So I'd suggest you get back to work and try to save our company. Remember, your name's on the door as well as mine."

The men faced each other, squared off as though about to challenge one another physically. David drew a deep breath. "I was afraid this would be an emotional topic for you, but, please Dad, give it—"

"I'm *not* being emotional." Arch's voice began to rise. "It's a matter of principle. Dolan Laboratories has been part of our family for three generations and we're not going to give it up now! Selling the company is too easy. Stay the course, David. That's always been the Dolan way."

David reached for his father's arm again, but the old man turned aside, out of his grasp. "Let's approach this like businessmen, Dad, not family."

Arch clenched his fists and pounded them on his thighs. "But we *are* family, and Dolan Laboratories *is* a family business! My father's business! Once my business! Now your business. Dolan. Dolan. Dolan. Goddamn it, son, don't you understand?"

"Yes, sir, I understand. You built a great company. No one can take that from you, but we've got to change our way of thinking."

Arch turned and started toward the house. "There's no sense talking about this anymore. And don't get any ideas about a proxy fight. Your mother and I still control the company, so what you and Ben and the bankers want doesn't add up to a hill of beans."

David took several long strides to catch his father and walked with him without speaking up the hill, side by side, separated by a few awkward feet. Arch climbed the steps to the terrace and sat heavily in a wrought-iron chair. David pulled a chair opposite him, sat and leaned forward, his sweat drenched shirt pressing to his back, his hands in front of his face as if in prayer. He waited a moment before speaking. "Dad, hear me out for a second; we're talking about the financial future of our company."

"Haven't I taught you anything?" his father said. He straightened in his chair and flicked a ladybug from the back of his hand. "This isn't about money, David. This is about history. About pride. Independence. The family name." He leaned forward and whispered, "Your brother wouldn't have quit on me."

David felt his stomach tighten. "Goddamn it, Dad, leave Arch out of this! I'm not quitting. I'm just . . ." He drew a deep breath and struggled to get back in control. He placed his hands on his knees. "Arch would have done exactly what I'm doing, and if you were still at the helm, so would you. It's the best thing for everyone involved."

"Well, to hell with everyone. How much do they need, anyway? I've made them all rich as Croesus as it is." Arch struggled to stand. He seemed less steady on his feet than usual. "Mark my words, your brother would have fought for our name, for our independence. Just the way he did in Vietnam."

David erupted from his chair, face to face with his father, barely a foot apart. "What's that mean?" he yelled. "Well? What the hell does that mean? I couldn't go. They wouldn't take me. Four-F. Remember?" He reached his trembling hands for his father to pull him close to him, to make him understand that he was doing what he thought best, what he was paid to do, to ask him—*just for once*—to give him the benefit of the doubt, but the old man stepped beyond his reach. "Dad, please, listen to me. You can't turn to Arch, and neither can I. And the last thing I'd ever do would be to sell out on you. We're all each other has to see this thing through. You're not going to let business come between us, are you?"

"I keep telling you, it's not about business," his father said, "so why don't you let me finish up a happy man?" He pushed by David and walked toward the house. David turned to follow him when both men stopped.

Elizabeth stood at the edge of the terrace holding a tray filled with glasses, plates, silverware and napkins. Her mouth was open wide as though she were calling for someone without a sound. Susan stood behind her, her hands on the older woman's slight shoulders. For an instant no one moved. Finally, Arch shuffled his large frame past the two women, pulled open the screen door and let it slam behind him as he disappeared into the house. David took the tray from his mother. "Oh, David," she said, "how did it come to this?"

He set the tray carefully on the porch dining table, and then put his hands over Susan's, now both holding tight to his mother's shoulders. "I think I caught him by surprise. I'll try to settle him down."

Inside the house, he stood in the library and called for his father. As his eyes adjusted from the bright glare of the midday sun to the darkness of the small room, he called again, and, while waiting for an answer, studied the row of photographs aligned across the bookshelf in front of him. It began with a picture of Susan, sitting cross-legged on a lawn, her skirt held over her knees with one arm, her other arm resting across the shoulders of a massive, dark-coated German shepherd that lay beside her.

A picture of their daughters, all apricot-blondes like their mother with rangy builds like his, followed. The teenagers, Samantha and Christi, are on all fours, straining to hold their heads up to look at the camera. Their younger sister, Charlotte, kneels on their backs, a hand on a shoulder of each. She is smiling her mother's broad smile, but her eyes are tight shut. The photograph always amused David because, a second after he took it, his older daughters collapsed, spilling Charlotte onto the lawn with shrieks of laughter.

The next was a studio photograph of Arch Jr. in his Marine dress blue uniform, his confidence and competence radiating through his pale blue eyes. David ran his finger along the top of the silver frame as though he were conducting a military inspection. "Hey, old buddy," he said aloud, "you're the one who should be in this mess, not me. I'm only here by default, and he'll never forget it."

His brother's photograph was followed by an empty space and then a picture of his parents taken at their fiftieth wedding anniversary celebration, a black-tie event held at Fox Hill. They are facing one another, holding each other's hands, beaming, and he thought how different they looked today; his father so disturbed and uncompromising, his mother worried and confused.

He noticed that the picture of him perched on the edge of the table in the boardroom at Dolan Laboratories, the photograph that was taken the day he was named Chairman and CEO of his family's business, was lying face down on the floor. He picked it up, blew dust from its glass and looked through the small window that faced out to the porch and watched Susan and his mother wrap their arms around each other, all the while Susan nodding and comforting his mother by patting her on the shoulder. At that moment he realized that his father was right, that this was about family, not about business, but he didn't have the slightest idea how to separate the two. The only thing he could think to do was stay his course, for he couldn't imagine how things could get much worse. He carefully replaced his picture on the bookshelf and called for his father once more, but still there was no answer.

CHAPTER 2

JJ Jennings and the maître d' at the Neal Street Restaurant were laughing and moving their hands as though they were juggling invisible objects while Bud Haney sat quietly, trying not to be seen or to interrupt, for he enjoyed studying JJ—the graceful sweeps of her hands, the animated way she talked, the way her smile seemed to welcome everyone. *I doubt she's ever met a stranger,* he thought. *She'd charm the balls off a brass monkey.* A moment more and JJ hooked the maître d's arm in hers and they hurried to Bud's table. He stood, buttoned his dark suit jacket and smoothed his hands over the flaps to his pockets to make sure they were in order. JJ patted the maître d' on the sleeve and spoke to him in Italian. When she turned to Bud, he put out his hand. "Sorry to call you so late in the day." Even though he'd lived in London for six years, he was still aware of how out of place his southern accent sounded and lowered his voice. "I reckon you had other plans tonight."

"Don't be silly," JJ said. "I'm glad you called."

Their waiter set a glass of wine in front of JJ and a beer in front of Bud. "I ordered a pinot grigio for you. That what you still drink?"

"Perfect," she said, and raised her glass. "Here's to a break from the routine."

He raised his glass to hers. "Don't be so sure. I think I'm about to mess up your life but good."

JJ sipped her wine and smiled. "Be my guest. My life could use a little messing up."

Bud reached for the black leather briefcase that sat on the floor beside his chair, unlatched its brass clasps and fished a periodical from it. "Look what's in this week's *Pink Sheet*." He handed it to JJ and pointed to the headline: **Dolan Laboratories Recalls Dolatriptan.**

JJ flinched slightly and straightened in her chair. "Have you talked with them?"

"Nope. I wanted to talk with you first, but this is pretty much the death knell for David and his family unless . . ." He paused. "Unless someone bails them out."

JJ studied the article for a moment. Bud thought there was an amused look in her eyes as she handed *The Pink Sheet* back to him. "And who might that white knight be? The mighty IPP under the leadership of its handsome, charismatic chief executive?"

Bud ignored her question. "My gut tells me that acquiring Dolan would be the right thing to do, but I wanted your assessment because David's a real good friend and I don't want that to color my thinking."

"Good enough to put your neck on the line for him?" JJ asked.

"Good enough to stick my neck way out for him," he answered, for David and he had worked side by side for fifteen years to make Dolan Laboratories something special and, along with David's father, had built the business to the twenty-eighth largest company on the *Forbes 500 Top Private Companies* list, making it larger than some more familiar names such as the Hearst publishing empire, the Gallo winery, LL Bean. Bud took a sip of his beer and added, "David and I have a special bond."

JJ beckoned to him with a smile, urging him to say more.

He hesitated. When he finally spoke, his voice was almost a whisper. "His brother was killed in Vietnam the same day I was shot down. Once David discovered this, from then on he called me the brother he once had." He waved his hands palms down, signaling that he wanted to drop the subject. "Let's just leave it that over time David, his wife and his kids, and his parents grew to mean a whole lot to me; they kind of made up for all those foster homes in Alabama." He studied his beer. "I only hope I mean as much to them."

"I'm sure you do," JJ said.

He looked up at her with a blank stare.

"Would you like to keep on talking about this?" she asked.

"No, ma'am. Enough of that."

"Okay," she said, then added, "I guess it'll have to be okay." She gave him what he had grown to think of as her banker's look. "Now down to business. Your Board and the investment community won't be interested in your personal motives, so give me a sound *business* reason to acquire Dolan Laboratories."

"Simple. Lomaxidine."

"Their new compound for memory loss and Alzheimer's?"

"You got it."

JJ raised her eyebrows. "You'd bet three—maybe even four—billion dollars on a drug that's yet to be approved?"

Bud ran his thumb down the side of his glass and looked directly at her. As he did, she smiled and he found himself smiling, too. "Why, yes, ma'am. It's being touted as Viagra for the brain. The hard part's going to be getting the family to agree to sell. David might be okay with it, but it's not what you'd call his father's favorite topic."

"Their problem, not yours," JJ said, and held up two fingers. "Reason number two?"

He couldn't help but notice her hands, how graceful they were without any jewelry. He thought they were just like her: stylish, yet without any frills. "We can use their sales forces to promote a number of our drugs while we're waiting for lo-maxidine to be approved."

"So far, so good." She raised a third, well-manicured finger. "Give me one more."

"It'll give us a rationale to change our registration from a British company to an American company."

"That again?" She inched her fork and knife back and forth. "Do you still really want to pursue that?"

"You sound surprised. I thought we both agreed it would put us on a more even footing when dealing with other American companies."

"Well . . ." She hesitated. "Yes . . . well . . . maybe . . . what I'm trying to say is I've thought about it a lot since, and I've come to the conclusion it could be very costly. Maybe too costly."

"Well, I think we ought to keep on studying it. It's something we've been trying to find a way to do for years, and it's something I'd like to do."

JJ looked down into her half-empty wine glass. Her question was barely audible. "And why is that again?"

"Come on, JJ, you know as well as I do. It would give me the opportunity to move back to the States."

She followed her wine glass with her eyes as she moved it in a small circle on the white linen tablecloth. "London would never be the same without you."

"London was doing just fine before I arrived and I'm sure it'll do just fine when I go home," he said. "But that's not what we're here to talk about. I'm trying to figure out if acquiring Dolan makes good business sense."

JJ reached for his hand and looked up at him. "London would be damn lonely without you," she whispered.

Bud sat for a moment, her hand covering his. Her touch was unfamiliar but comforting. Gently, he lifted her hand and set it on the table, pressing down on it to keep it in place but also to feel her touch for a moment longer. He slipped his hands slowly into his jacket pockets and said, "Hey, this isn't about where I hang my hat. What I need to know from you is, should we make a bid for Dolan? If you would, just give me a simple 'yes' or 'no.'"

"Where would you go?" she asked. "Back to Alabama? To Hope Hull?"

Bud shook his head. "No more, JJ. Please, no more."

She waved at their waiter and signaled for the check.

"What in the Sam Hill are you doing?" he asked.

"Trying to figure out whether buying Dolan Laboratories is a smart thing for you—for IPP—to do." She reached for her purse. "I need some time to think about it; to discuss it with my colleagues. I'll be back to you late tomorrow."

The waiter placed the bill in a maroon leather folder in front of Bud. JJ reached across the table, pulled the folder to her and slipped her credit card inside it. "And what are you doing now?" he said. "I invited *you* to dinner."

JJ looked at him and gave him what he thought was a pained smile. "When it's your turn to buy, it'll be when we're together on a personal basis." Bud had never seen the look that followed. He sensed that she could see right through him, see things he didn't understand—maybe things he didn't want her to see—and he shifted slightly in his chair. "You know what I'm talking about here? Boy meets girl—stuff like that. But until then, until we can talk about something other than business—when you're ready to give me more than just your name, rank, service number and date of—"

He pushed his hands toward her. "Whoa! That kind of talk is out of bounds."

"With you, talking about *anything* personal is out of bounds."

Bud folded his arms across his chest. "Maybe. Maybe not. But I told you long ago that there are some things I don't ever want to be reminded of, some things I'm trying every day to forget. And I don't need you reciting the Code of Conduct to stir things up especially when I'm trying to talk some sense with you about buying Dolan—"

"Code of conduct?" JJ interrupted. "Is that what you call it? Well, can't you every once in a while drop all that code of conduct stuff? You've been out of the Navy for twenty-five years. You're no longer a prisoner, Buddy, but you *are* all alone in a world where most people rely on their friends—on relationships. So can't you just for once let your guard down and talk with me about something other than doing deals? Can't you just for once treat me like a friend—maybe even like a member of the opposite sex—rather than your investment banker? What could possibly be wrong with that? What code could that possibly violate?"

Bud studied her face. She was a colleague whom he respected and admired and, most important of all, trusted more than anyone else—but now he saw a passion he had never seen before and a caring for him personally that made him uncomfortable. "I guess I owe you an apology, but you know as well as anyone that I'm a private guy and I've got a couple of rules I try never to break."

He had outlined those rules in his first meeting with her after she was given the lead role on the IPP account at Gilbert-Beard. He had told her that he never mixed business with pleasure and that he tried never to talk or think about Vietnam. In an unguarded moment—one he later regretted—he told her that he had talked about Vietnam a great deal right after he was freed because the doctors told him it would help him get rid of his nightmares, but that once they'd pretty much disappeared he'd tried to put the whole experience behind him, and that most times it worked, but sometimes he got all stirred up without any warning. And he confessed to her that being a prisoner for five years had put him behind his peers, not only in the Navy but in business as well, and he'd been running hard to catch up ever since.

"No need to apologize," she said. "I should have known better." She drew a deep breath. "So, in my capacity as your investment banker, I'm picking up the check. And now, if you'll excuse me, I'd better go home and get down to work."

He followed her as she weaved through the tables to the door of the restaurant. People entering were shaking water off their umbrellas and stamping their shoes. "Come on, JJ," he said, "It's raining cats and dogs. I'll give you a lift home."

"No need for that. I'll take a cab."

"Not on my watch." He stepped to the doorway, looked up and down the narrow street, and waved an open hand. Halfway up the block the lights of a black sedan blinked on and off. He stepped back and took her firmly by the arm and when his car pulled in front of the restaurant opened its door and hurried her in out of the rain. "It's a good thing you waited, Steve," he said to his driver. "Miss Jennings has got to get home to do some work for us."

During the half-hour drive to JJ's flat, Bud and she sat in silence, staring out their respective windows at the rain and heavy London traffic. When they stopped, she fished her keys from her purse, leaned forward and patted the driver on the shoulder. "Please, Steve, don't get out. I'll make a dash for it." She rested her hand on the door handle and turned to Bud.

From the glow of the streetlight, and from the rain running down the car windshield—the Mercedes' large single wiper rhythmically clearing it back and forth—blotches of shadow moved across the back seat, blemishing her cream-colored skin with its faint freckles, causing her open features to look as if they had cracked and shifted in places—one instant her broad mouth in shadow, the next drawn tight without the hint of a smile; one moment her large brown eyes hidden, then both visible, the watery reflections making it appear as though they were filled with tears. "Don't worry, Mr. Haney, you can relax," she said. "I know my role and tomorrow I'll be the consummate professional once again. I'm sorry about my hurtful comments. I was hoping it wasn't a working dinner. I guess I got my signals crossed."

Bud reached for her, to tell her that they could talk about the boy-girl stuff some other time, but she was gone and all he could do was watch as she ran up a short flight of steps, quickly unlock the outer door to her building and disappear out of the rain. "God help us," he said under his breath. "God help the two of us."

Once under way again, his driver interrupted his thoughts. "Miss Jennings was her usual, smashing self this evening, Mr. Haney."

Bud looked up and saw Steve smiling at him in the rearview mirror. "She's a damn good banker and a real hard worker," he said. "And I've just given her one hell of an important assignment."

"I understand," his driver said.

Bud thought there was a knowing tone to Steve's voice. "Just exactly *what* do you understand?"

"That Miss Jennings is an excellent banker and works very hard on the company's behalf. On very important issues, I should add."

"That's good, Steve." He smiled. "You've got it just right. She's one hell of a banker and a real hard worker; nothing more, nothing less."

"Certainly, sir."

The Mercedes came to a stop in front of a connected row of three-story white houses on Eaton Terrace. Bud opened the door a crack and said, "See you tomorrow morning at seven-thirty. Have a good night."

"And you, Mr. Haney."

He stepped from the car, shut the door and then tapped a knuckle on the front window. The glass slowly slipped down and Steve leaned across the seat toward him. "Yes, sir?"

Bud reached through the open window and shook his driver's hand. "We see a lot of stuff together, don't we, Steve?"

"We certainly do, Mr. Haney."

"Well, good night," Bud said again. "And thanks for the chat."

A quizzical look crossed his driver's face. "Sir?"

"I said thanks for the chat."

"Oh. Certainly, sir. My pleasure, sir."

Bud watched as the window slid to a close and the dark car pulled away from the curb. He tried to order his thoughts and dismiss what he was feeling for, to his way of thinking, feeling had no place in his work. He told himself that he had more important things to worry about than his relationship with his investment banker, like a three- to four-billion dollar decision, and wondered, *Do I or don't I step in and save David's bacon and bet the ranch on lomaxidine?*

He turned and climbed the stairs to the entrance to number thirty-three. As he drew his keys from his pocket, he thought his competitors must be wrestling with the same questions, that they all had the capacity to buy Dolan, just the way IPP did. He unlocked the bottom lock and inserted his key in the top lock. Over his shoulder he caught a glimpse of a woman hurrying down the sidewalk, her dark hair matted from the rain. For a moment he thought it was JJ and turned to tell her that he'd like to talk, but it was his neighbor at number thirty-seven. "Not fit for man nor beast, is it Bud?" she called as she unlocked her door.

"No, ma'am, it isn't." He shook his head as though he were shaking water from his ears, trying to shake away his thoughts of JJ. "Focus, old son," he muttered. "This deal could make or break you."

CHAPTER 3

The modest boardroom of Dolan Laboratories sits on the second floor of the company's two-story, red brick headquarters; a bright, cream-colored room that overlooks the Dolan Research Campus, it welcomes the early fall sunlight. Hanging on its north wall is a portrait of a bald man with an angular face and an amused gaze in his blue eyes, eyes that follow visitors as they move about the room. A small brass plate at the bottom of the frame gleams beneath the muted painting: *Our Founder. David Justice Dolan. b1893—d1956.*

A portrait of a man dressed in a solid gray suit, chalk-white shirt and a red, gold and blue regimental-striped bow tie hangs on the facing wall. The subject is seated in a maroon leather chair, his forearms and large hands resting on its arms. He is in profile and appears to be focused on something in the distance. With his sharply turned-down nose and short-cropped white hair, he has the look of a bird of prey watching and waiting. The brass plate beneath this portrait reads: *Archibald Dolan Sr., Chairman and Chief Executive Officer. 1956—1993.*

34

Large aerial photographs of Dolan Laboratories' key overseas manufacturing sites in Puerto Rico, Ireland and Belgium cover much of the west wall. A narrow oval table with a highly polished, mahogany finish and a dozen gray leather chairs sits in the middle of the room.

As David studied each of his directors—*or are they family members?*—he realized he would be addressing a small group of people who epitomized one of the best-kept secrets about real wealth in America, for no one, except a handful of trusted advisors and the IRS, had any idea how rich many of the family members of privately held companies were. The fact that the Dolan Family was about to debate whether or not to sell their company for four billion dollars, making David—*the low man on the family totem pole*—worth $280 million, caused him to shake his head, for he felt it was an absurd amount of money for any individual to be worth. But, on the other side of the ledger, he had begun to view it as his "blood money," his compensation for all the pain the recall of Dolatriptan—and his father—were causing him; compensation for devoting his adult life to Dolan Laboratories. He smiled toward his father who was seated in his usual place at the opposite end of the table but Arch stared straight ahead, avoiding eye contact with him and the rest of his family. *Dad? Not today,* David thought. *Today he's my majority shareholder—owns thirty-eight percent of the company—and if he resists the deal I'm about to propose he'll be standing in the way of a payout of over one and a half billion dollars.*

He glanced at his mother who owned thirteen percent through gifts from his father whom she sat next to—*almost obediently,* David thought—chatting amiably with each family member while waiting for the meeting to begin. *Mom's stake's a little more than $500 million. Together, not only do she and Dad control the company, they're worth more than two billion dollars. Not too many people these days would turn down that kind of windfall.*

Benjamin Dolan, David's uncle, who owned seventeen percent of the company equaling $680 million, sat in one of the center chairs and gazed out the long expanse of glass and then smiled at his older brother and said, "Arch, we open the season against Cornell tomorrow."

"Princeton football? It bores me to tears," Arch said.

Sarah Dolan Howe, who owned an equal share with her brother Ben, sat opposite him, needle pointing a brightly colored picture of a hippopotamus, a present for a grandchild. She raised an eyebrow. "Oh really? But Arch, in your day you were *so* good."

"The game's changed," Arch said, still staring straight ahead.

Mike McPartland from JP Morgan was seated next to Sarah Howe. He and his bank represented trusts for numerous cousins and relatives of the Dolan family, not to mention David and Susan's three daughters. Bespectacled and cherubic-looking, McPartland sipped coffee from a green and black Starbucks cup, absent-mindedly wiping his mouth with a large white handkerchief and studying a neatly organized stack of papers in front of him. He looked up occasionally, smiling at anything anybody had to say. When he noticed David looking at him, he smiled once again and turned his hands palms up as though he were asking what more there was to wait for, signaling that the time had come.

David stood, shifted his weight to his left leg to ease the pressure on his right hip, and looked once more at each of the five people seated around the table, trying to read their moods, trying to get his bearings. "I'm sorry to call you into the office on such short notice, but, as you know, I have some news that affects all of—"

"Get on with it," Arch blurted out. "The whole thing's academic anyway."

"Hush, dear," Elizabeth said. "Let's hear what David has to say."

Arch shook his head and lowered his eyes as David said, "I wanted to discuss our problem—perhaps more optimistically our opportunity—as a family *and* as shareholders in Dolan Laboratories." He paused and looked at his father, hoping for some sign of acknowledgment, but Arch refused to look up and David pushed on, dispirited but believing he knew what was right, what he was obliged to do. He took a deep breath, exhaled it slowly and, beginning with the call from the FDA, started to outline the events that had led to this meeting.

"In the past when something like this happened," his father interrupted, "we'd just get up, brush ourselves off and find another drug." He turned a yellow wood pencil in his hands. "That's always been the Dolan way—to stay the course. At least up until now."

David felt his face redden and started to challenge his father, then caught himself. "Dad's right, and for the last two years we've been doing exactly what he's suggesting. But it's a lot like Princeton football. The game's changed."

Those who began to smile were brought up short by a sharp crack as Arch snapped the pencil he'd been twisting. "Nonsense," he said and stared at his hands and the jagged yellow halves of the pencil.

David continued, determined to meet his obligations as their company's chief executive. "And while our long-term drug pipeline is very promising, especially with lomaxidine, we've been unable to acquire rights to a drug to fill the gap left by Dolatriptan. As a result I've determined that it's in the family's best interest—*and* the company's best interest—to explore partnering with another company."

"Is that what you call it?" Arch stood; spittle glistening at the corners of his mouth. "Call a spade a spade, David; that's the boss's job. It's not partnering, it's selling out. Selling our family business, our family's name." He stared at his brother and then his sister. "Your name, Ben. And yours, Sarah. And mine." He swung his left arm over his wife's head and pointed to the portrait of his father. "His name, too, for Christ's sake!" His eyes darted from one family member to another. "What does a family have left after it's sold its name? Is there anything more sacred?" He looked at David and leaned over the table toward him and whispered hoarsely, "It's your brother's name. It's your name. Please, don't push this any further." He sat heavily, crossed his arms, and then let his hands slide to his lap. He hung his head, resting his chin on his chest. Almost inaudibly he said, "We've already lost one Dolan. If we sell the company, there'll be nothing left for any of us. I'm too tired to keep on fighting, David. You've got to save it for me. That's the least you can do."

Elizabeth reached for her husband's hand. At first he pulled it away, then eased it toward her. Her small pale hand reached again, found Arch's once powerful claw and squeezed it gently. She looked up at David and smiled. "Finish what you have to say."

He said the last point he wanted to make was that he had approached Bud Haney about a partnership of some kind. When he mentioned Haney's name, Sarah Howe said, "I always liked that young man."

All but Arch nodded in agreement, and David said he had chosen Bud and his company for that very reason. "He's a great friend and knows our family and our business. More important, he's the one person in the industry I can trust. He's offered four billion dollars—in cash—to acquire your company." He looked at his father, who continued to sit with his chin on his chest. "And, Dad, they've agreed to call the new company IPP-Dolan."

"A hollow victory," Arch muttered.

David realized then that there was absolutely no hope, that

his father was unreachable, but made his last point. "And Bud has asked his lawyers to research whether or not the new company can be based in the US, perhaps right here in Princeton."

"You're missing the point," his father said. "This isn't about what Bud Haney wants. It's about what we want. Four billion dollars? Our name and our business are worth one hell of a lot more than four billion dollars!"

"But, Arch," Sarah Howe said, "some of us want the money!"

David thought his aunt was oblivious to the withering look her brother gave her and added hurriedly, "If you have any questions, let's discuss them now."

The man from the Morgan Bank waved his hand at David, who nodded at him with an audible sigh of relief. He was glad it was McPartland—*anyone, at this point, but Dad*—who wanted to discuss his proposition.

McPartland surprised David and directed his comments to his father. "Arch, I realize what David is recommending is difficult for you. In many ways it's difficult for me, too, and for all of us at Morgan. You hired our bank forty-three years ago and we've always taken great pride in having you as a client. But, I know David feels it's in the best interest of the family *and* the company to find a friendly buyer, and I agree wholeheartedly. And I think the price he's negotiated is a fair value for your company so I believe I'm obligated to the beneficiaries of the trusts I oversee to vote Morgan's shares in line with David's proposal."

Arch looked up and stared at McPartland. "How much do you represent, Mike? Eight percent? Small potatoes. That still leaves you forty-three percent short of a majority."

"Are we taking a vote already?" Sarah Howe asked.

"Only if you're ready to," David said.

"I do have a question," Ben Dolan said. "What happens to you, David, if we approve this offer?"

"I'll work for Bud as his Chief Operating Officer." He looked at his father. "As COO I'll be able to make sure that the Dolan employees are given a fair chance in the new company."

"Why, I think that's wonderful. Don't you, Arch?" his sister asked.

Arch simply shook his head.

"Well, I think it's wonderful," she said, "and I vote my shares with David's proposal. Frankly, I can't wait to spend some of the proceeds!"

Ben Dolan nodded at David. "You have my vote, too."

"This is nonsense!" Arch said. "Absolute nonsense, Ben, and you know it. You all can vote and vote and vote until you're blue in the face, but you can't get a majority, so what's the use?"

David looked at his father. "Dad, for the record, I, too, vote my shares in favor of selling our company."

"That's it?" Arch said with a laugh. "Forty-nine percent in favor. Fifty-one percent against. Well, you can all go home now. My business is not for sale."

David was at a loss for words. He had done what he thought he must do, even though he realized that what he had recommended would never come to pass. But he had hoped there would be some discussion, perhaps even some compromise, at least some indication from his father that he thought what he was recommending was a legitimate approach. He had hoped for some healing. But now he had lost for good. He had done what he had thought was right, and had lost. *Thank God it's Bud Haney I have to explain this to. No one else would understand.* "Well, everyone," he said quietly, "if there are no further questions or issues you'd like to discuss . . ." He hesitated. "No other business . . ." He paused again. "Then the meeting is adjourned."

Sarah Howe began to pack her needlepoint in a large chintz bag and McPartland stood and was pulling on his jacket when David's mother startled him and all the others. "Not just yet, please. I'd like to say something." She shifted in her chair and faced her husband. "Arch, there's no way anyone can sell the Dolan name. That's impossible. It's yours and mine and all of ours to keep—forever. But the company is different. Yes, it bears your father's name, but he's long gone, and we remember him for the kind of man he was, not for the company he founded. So I ask you, dear Arch, how do *you* want to be remembered? With your name on a company that failed because in the end you were too proud to manage it like a business? Or do you want to be remembered as the man who built Dolan Laboratories to great heights and then, when the time was right, sold it to strengthen it even more?

"This whole thing is wrong, Arch. It's come between you and your only son, and between you and your brother. It's pulling our family apart. And for what? Foolish, stubborn, competitive family pride? Or because a drug is being recalled? None are more important than our family." Her look was steady. "You've already lost one son. God help us, don't lose another. Let's you and I concentrate on what we've nurtured at Fox Hill, and let someone else worry about the business for a change."

Arch swiveled his chair and stared at Elizabeth in disbelief. "Are you selling out on me, too?"

"No, dear, not selling out on you. I'm doing something far more important than selling a company. I'm trying to cut away a cancer from our family before it spreads and kills us all." She placed her small hands in her lap and rubbed them together as though she were kneading dough. There were no audible sobs, no visible heaves, but tears slid slowly down her delicately defined, pale cheeks. She looked at David, and then turned to her husband of fifty-seven years, a look of disbelief still on his face. "Arch, I'm voting my shares with David's proposal to put an end to all of this."

No one spoke or moved. The only sound David could hear was the gentle push of the air conditioning system. A slight wave of nausea came over him. *What in God's name have I just done? Sold my family's business—the family name and all that goes with it—and driven a wedge between my father and me, and now maybe a wedge between my mother and father; that's what I've done. And all in the name of good management. Sixty-six years of being a proud, successful, independent family-held business down the drain in a heartbeat. I never really thought it would happen like this.*

His father pushed himself from his chair and walked the length of the table and David stepped aside to make room for him to pass. As Arch reached for the door handle, he turned and looked at Elizabeth. "Go ahead, sell the goddamned business if you must. It's your decision, not mine, and seeing that I'm not needed here anymore, I'd like to go home and take the dog for a walk around Fox Hill, unless you think I should sell that, too."

The majority shareholders of Dolan Laboratories watched as their family business's chief executive for thirty-eight years, brother to two of them, husband to one, father to another, shuffled, stooped and beaten, out of the room. David heard him cough, and then heard a door slam.

Elizabeth collected her purse and followed her husband, her short, sure steps carrying her quickly the length of the table and out the room.

"David, go with your dad," his uncle said. "Help your mother help him get over this, because she's right; it's not about selling a business, it's about family and your father needs you now more than you think. In time, I think he'll come around."

David nodded at his uncle, but doubted if he was right. *It will kill him first,* he thought. *And all because of me.*

CHAPTER 4

"Americans."

Richard Beecroft didn't look at his wife when he said it. Instead, he lowered his head as he walked and stared at the gravel path beneath his booted feet, his hands clasped behind his back, his torso canted forward. Fiona walked on his left, occasionally skipping to keep up, while Cider, their yellow Labrador retriever, trotted at heel on Richard's right.

The Beecrofts were engaged in the routine they had followed every Sunday since their marriage two months before: starting at half-past ten in the morning, they walked a little more than a mile over country lanes and footpaths to St. Andrew's Anglican Church in Nether Wallop. After having made their presence known and having endured the eleven o'clock service, they walked briskly back to White Gate Cottage, their small, thatched-roof retreat in Over Wallop, where Richard would work in the garden until two, eat a light lunch accompanied by two cups of dark tea and, punctually at three o'clock, drive back to their home in London, arriving no later than half-past four. There he would spend the rest of the afternoon and evening preparing for the press of business that lay ahead of him in the upcoming week.

He was dressed as he was every Sunday: olive corduroy trousers tucked inside dark green Wellington boots; a tattersall shirt and solid maroon necktie covered by a battered Barbour jacket—brownish-green and badly in need of a waxing—and a herringbone tweed cap pulled well down his forehead.

At thirty-seven, Fiona was almost twenty years younger than Richard. His long strides caused her to walk hurriedly to keep pace; his height requiring that she look up to address him. As a result, she stumbled occasionally in her high-heeled leather boots. She wore clothes similar to her husband's, but chosen for a different effect. Her tailored olive slacks were worn outside her Ferragamo boots and clung to her thighs and buttocks. Her Barbour was in the same state of disrepair as Richard's but was worn open to give a hint of the silk and cashmere and full breasts beneath it. She had tied a pale blue scarf over her wavy blonde hair to keep it in place and compliment her large blue eyes.

Richard muttered "Americans" a second time, for since the Dolan family had begun the process of selling their company to IPP, Americans were very much at the heart of his problem. But the American in question this morning was a senior executive with Goldman Sachs, who—*as was his habit,* Richard thought—was talking baby talk to his Yorkshire terrier. Fiona called to his wife to arrange a game of tennis. They called back and forth as though they were already in the midst of a rally. When they had settled it—"Queen's Club, Tuesday at ten"—Fiona and the American couple waved good-bye. Richard simply raised the index finger of his right hand to the bill of his tweed cap and kept walking, for his mind was in his boardroom.

When the Beecrofts had moved out of earshot of the Americans, Fiona pressed her chest against Richard's arm. "Don't be too hard on them. They're trying so desperately to fit in. At least he's chucked driving the Bentley."

"Oh?" Richard said. "Next they should get a proper dog."

They walked from the churchyard, mingling with several of their country neighbors, all people who, like them, lived in London during the week and retreated to their cottages for the weekend. An elderly couple stopped to say hello. The husband, James Beery, a member of the European Parliament and desperate to stay on Richard's good side, asked when he and Richard might get together. Richard feigned to be unaware of their greeting and clucked at Cider and hurried past them. Beery asked a second time and Richard, with Fiona smiling and waving, called back over his shoulder, "Call me midweek, if you don't mind."

The Beecrofts walked swiftly over the narrow footpath without speaking. Finally, Fiona asked how his week was taking shape. "Better than last, I hope," she said.

"Quite civilized, actually. Quite orderly and routine."

"Something always seems to happen to change that." She gave her husband a quick, knowing smile for she had been his secretary for five years before marrying him and knew how unpredictable it was to be Chairman and Chief Executive Officer of one of Britain's largest companies. "I hope you've marked your diary that we're going to the opera with the Lynches on Thursday night."

Richard forced a brief smile. "We do seem to be seeing a lot of Americans lately. Don't we have any English friends anymore? Or have they all abandoned me?"

"The worst is behind us," she said.

He opened the white gate their cottage was named for and as Fiona slipped past him studied the perfectly rounded bottom of her buttocks. "Was there anything in *The Times* this morning?"

"I don't know," she said over her shoulder, "and I don't care."

"Don't care or afraid to look?"

She said she no longer cared. "I'm fine as long as you promise you'll never let it happen again."

The phone rang as they finished pulling off their boots and hanging their Barbours in the small mudroom behind their kitchen. Richard wiped Cider's muddy paws with a dark-stained towel while Fiona padded into the kitchen in her stockinged feet to answer the phone. She quickly clasped her hand over the mouthpiece. "It's for you." She pulled the receiver against her shoulder and lowered her voice. "It sounds like someone's secretary. I thought we agreed you wouldn't take any business calls when we were here."

Richard took the phone and wrapped his hand over the mouthpiece. "I'll be brief," he said, and then spoke into the phone and asked who was calling.

A woman's voice answered, "It's Secretary Benson. If you would, sir, please hold for just a moment."

Richard put both hands over the mouthpiece and shook the phone in front of him in short, jerky motions to get Fiona's attention. "This may take a moment. It's Peter Benson."

Fiona gave him a worried look. "What in God's name could he want on a Sunday morning?"

A man's voice on the other end of the line interrupted them. "Richard, I'm sorry to bother you on a Sunday, but we have a problem of some urgency that I'd hoped you might be able to help us with."

"A problem, Peter? We?"

Peter Benson, the Secretary of State for the Department of Trade and Industry, cleared his throat. "I'm sure you know that IPP is in merger discussions with an American firm."

"Dolan Laboratories," Richard said.

"Spot on." The Secretary cleared his throat again. "We're told they're very close to an agreement, and our sources also tell us that one of the terms of that agreement is that the merged company will be domiciled in America. As I'm sure you've read, *The Times* has already started to beat the drum about IPP falling into foreign hands." There was an edge to Benson's voice that told Richard to keep his guard up. "Richard, do you see where this is headed?" Benson asked.

"Frankly, no. Where IPP is domiciled is of little concern to me."

"All well and good for you, Richard, but it's a *great* concern to us," the Secretary said.

"And *who*, exactly, is *us*?"

"You know as well as I do." Benson paused for a second. "Actually, Richard, the Prime Minister asked me to place this call."

"Oh, and how does he think I can help?"

"Between you and me, he's concerned about losing another blue-chipper to foreign ownership," Benson answered. "The media will hammer away that our role on the world stage is being diminished even further. Moreover, at the end of the day, we'll have lost thousands more jobs as well. We're being back-footed here, Richard, and it will make us look quite bad."

"Those jobs will be lost no matter where the company is domiciled," Richard said. "That's part of the rationale—"

The Secretary sighed dismissively. "No matter, the list of disappearing companies is becoming way too long for the PM's taste. Just look at automotives. Jaguar to Ford. Rover to BMW. And now, of all things, Rolls Royce and Bentley to Volkswagen. He's complaining that he can no longer be driven about in an English-made car."

Fiona quietly set a cup of tea on the counter by Richard's side. "I'm going to draw a bath," she whispered and traced a finger lightly through his hair and down his neck. "Join me?" she asked, and pulled him toward her by his free hand.

He shook his head.

"Are you still there, Richard?"

"Just a moment," he said. He looked at Fiona and shrugged his shoulders.

She lifted his index finger, closed her mouth over it, rolled her tongue around it and bit it gently before slowly drawing away. "You don't know what you'll be missing."

"Richard, am I interrupting something?"

Richard cleared his throat and watched Fiona hurry out of the kitchen and up the narrow stairs. "Sorry. You were saying . . ."

The Secretary's words came slowly over the phone. "Richard, how does the Prime Minister explain to the public that IPP's become an American company?"

"A good question, but one I'm sure—"

"Good Lord, man, it's more than a good question! It's a bloody PR nightmare. If this deal goes through, it will make us look bad, and the Prime Minister is sick of it and so am I."

A smile crossed Richard's face. He liked thinking of Peter Benson in a difficult position. "How can I help?" His smile lingered as he sipped his tea and waited for the Secretary to answer.

Benson's reply caused him to straighten. "The Prime Minister was wondering if you would step in."

"Step in?"

"And why not, might I ask? Someone quite close to your company has told us that your Board is all for it, that it could make you the largest pharmaceutical company in the world."

"Not could, but would," Richard said quickly. *A leak on my*

Board to 10 Downing Street? Good Lord, that's all I need. He ran a hand through his hair. "It's out of the question."

"Is there a problem?"

Richard picked up his teacup and set it back on the counter. The last thing he wanted was another public battle that could lead to further publicity for him and Fiona for there was still an occasional article in the press—usually planted by his ex-wife and one of London's leading PR firms—about his affair with Fiona that had led to his contentious divorce. "All I'm at liberty to say is that my Board and I think it would be a good strategic move, but I can't construct a scenario that I think would be acceptable to IPP."

"Have you considered a take-over?" the Secretary asked.

"The Secretary of State for the Department of Trade and Industry suggesting a hostile take-over? My God, man, you really *must* be under a lot of pressure."

"Suggesting's not my job," Benson said. "I simply ask questions, for thoroughness."

"I see. Well, for thoroughness . . ." He paused, thinking what a snake Benson was. "We considered the idea and dismissed it. The price would be seventy billion pounds, or more."

"In for a penny, in for a pound," the Secretary said. "Surely you can raise the capital, and you'll have our full support." Richard closed his eyes and shook his head. "And, if you should step in," Benson continued, "we'll make sure that the press knows you have our blessing. But, might I suggest that, if you don't take action, the pundits will be less than kind with you and—"

"Is that a threat?" Richard asked.

"Hold on. I'm just going around the houses for thoroughness' sake, and I might add that the Prime Minister has already had a conversation with Her Majesty and she supports his logic."

Richard looked down at his yellow-stockinged feet, and rubbed his right arch over the bridge of his left foot. He was beginning to feel trapped, sensing there was more at stake than what was being discussed. "Peter, you're not giving me much of a choice here, but I can't emphasize enough that I don't need another go in the press."

"Richard, I think you're preoccupied by the media," Benson said. "There are plenty of divorces that have become front page fun."

Richard laughed. "*I'm* preoccupied by the media?"

"I've taken enough of your time," Benson said. "What do you say?"

Richard sipped his tea and looked through the amber liquid to the bottom of the cup, as though he might find his answer there.

Benson pressed harder. "If you cooperate, I'm told that little tap on the shoulder will soon follow."

That little tap on the shoulder? Those bastards! He sighed. "I'll let you know our decision within forty-eight hours."

"We knew we could count on you. None of us can afford to appear indifferent on this matter. Cheers for now."

Richard heard a click as the Secretary hung up. He stared at the phone as though it were a foreign object. *Count on me? That little tap on the shoulder? So this is what it's going to take to get my knighthood.* He slammed the phone on its cradle and stared through a small, lead-framed window, watching the cold November rain fall on his garden, shifting his weight from one yellow-stockinged foot to the other. *If it weren't for the media raising the Fiona bit, what harm would it do to take one more look? Perhaps Haney would agree if I promise him the top job. Perhaps my Board's right.* At the thought of his Board, once again he worried that they might be losing confidence in him over his reluctance to follow their counsel. *Perhaps there is a way to structure a deal that would be acceptable. Perhaps the media would let me alone.*

While he knew that it was a gamble, the pressure—first from his Board, and now from the Prime Minister—made him extremely uncomfortable, but what kept coming back to haunt him was the additional cost to his reputation if he got it wrong. His divorce and his marrying Fiona, who in her early twenties had posed as a Page Three Girl in *The Galaxy,* had made him the frequent brunt of jokes by business writers, society editors and cartoonists. A picture on the cover of *The Mirror* the day after their wedding with the headline "Bust Married!" was only the beginning, and he was worried that leading a hostile raid on one of Britain's oldest companies would bring the media down upon him once again. But now, his knighthood—a dream he'd worked toward for thirty years—stood in the balance. "Bloody hell," he said aloud, "there must be another way." *Preoccupied with all of this? I damn well am, and for good reason.*

He turned as he heard Fiona behind him. She wore a bathrobe wrapped loosely around her. "What did Peter want? It sounded a bit ugly."

"The PM wants me to step in with IPP before they become an American company."

"But you went through all that last week with the Board," she said. "And they agreed with you."

"Apparently not all. One of them has leaked our discussions to Downing Street and now they're turning up the heat."

"No. No more, Richard. Not a battle. No more of me in the press," Fiona pleaded. "I can't stand any more of it."

"Me neither." He paused and looked down at his wife who had moved against him. He took her by the shoulders with both hands, leaned slightly forward and stared into her large blue eyes. "They're using my knighthood as the incentive."

"That's not fair. It means too much to you."

"You mean, to *us*."

"Of course I mean to us. I dream about it almost every day. Sir Richard and Lady Beecroft. It sounds so lovely. It's what I want. It's where I thought we were headed."

"Well, perhaps there's a way to satisfy them all and get what I—I mean, what we—want."

Fiona slid her arms around her husband's waist and pressed against him. "Promise me no matter what you do, you'll keep me out of the limelight. Promise?"

"Maybe there's a way around it," he said. His mind already had him racing up the A303, heading back home to London, when Fiona began to move slowly across him. "Maybe it's time Bud Haney and I tried to sort it all out. I can't do it without him."

"Not now," Fiona whispered. "No more." She took his hand and guided it inside the top of her robe. He brushed his fingers lightly over her rigid nipples and felt himself swelling against his corduroys. He wrapped his other arm around Fiona's back and looked down at his watch to determine when he'd be at work in London, but could no longer concentrate on his schedule, or on Bud Haney and IPP, or his Board of Directors, or the Prime Minister's requests. He untied her robe and pulled it off her shoulders. *When she's like this, she's worth all the trouble she's caused me.* He reached under her arms and lifted her, she wrapping her legs around his waist, he folding his arms behind her to hold her tight against him.

Fiona smiled, moistened her parted lips and cupped her breasts together and upward in her well-known Page Three pose. *Well, in for a penny, in for a pound,* Richard thought as he lowered her buttocks and back on the small kitchen table, just as he had that evening four years before when he had eased her onto the cool, smooth table in the Whitecliff boardroom.

"Wouldn't *HELLO!* just love to see this," Fiona said as she tugged at Richard's belt and zipper and then guided him to her. "I can see the headline now: Sir Richard and Lady Beecroft at play in their country cottage."

"Hush," Richard said, clamping his hand over her mouth. "Don't spoil it. Your time will come."

CHAPTER 5

Bud Haney slipped his feet from his desk and walked across a large expanse of rich green carpet, rolling his tasseled black loafers from heel to toe with each step. At the window, he rested his hands on the sill, placed one foot in front of the other and began stretching his hamstrings. He and his Chief Financial Officer, Nigel Finch-Hatton, had been reviewing the updated projections for DIP—IPP's code name for the proposed acquisition of Dolan Laboratories—and he was finding it hard to concentrate. He had arrived in London early in the morning, having taken the overnight flight from New York, and was fighting jet lag.

He checked his watch. *Almost six o'clock. Feel like I was rode hard and put away wet.* He continued to stretch and looked out the window. "Damn, Nigel," he said, "doesn't it ever do anything but rain in your country?"

Nigel looked at his boss, trying as always, Bud thought, to read his mood and said, "Well, Bud, I think that's enough for this evening." He stacked his papers neatly in front of him, capped his pen and clipped it inside his dark suit jacket, and assured his boss that the due diligence process with Dolan was going well, that they would be ready to close their deal by the end of the week.

That was all Bud needed to hear. He was convinced that acquiring Dolan Laboratories and the rights to lomaxidine was a smart move, and he smiled at the thought of working with David Dolan once again. He could see the future that he had sculptured, and he liked what he saw. He would be in charge of an ever-growing pharmaceutical empire, a multinational corporation with annual sales soon to exceed $15 billion. He was strengthening IPP's future and, with it, his own future as well. *My shareholders are happy,* he thought, *and so's my Board. Old son, you're in high cotton.*

He strolled back to his desk and glanced at the figures once more. "If that's all you've got for me Nigel, let's call it a day. I'm going to tidy up here a bit and head on home."

As he spoke, his phone blinked and buzzed. He looked at his secretary through the glass front to his office. She mouthed "sorry," and put her hands together in prayer for him to answer her buzz. He pressed the button on his phone.

"It's Dr. Beecroft," she said. "I told him you were in a meeting, but he insisted I interrupt. Shall I put him through?"

Bud nodded at Nigel, who shrugged his narrow shoulders, pushed his slight frame from his chair and slipped out of the office. "Okay, Jo, put him through," he said. *Dr. Mickey Mouse? What in hell is he calling about at this hour?*

When his phone rang, he punched the speaker button. "Hey, Richard. You calling to raise more money for the Royal Opera House?"

"This is a business call," Richard answered, "and a rather important one at that. I think it would be a good idea if we got together."

Bud waited for him to say more. When he didn't, Bud broke the silence and suggested that their secretaries set up a meeting, perhaps in two or three weeks' time, after the Dolan deal was out of the way.

"Obviously you don't understand," Richard said. "I'm suggesting we meet to discuss *our companies* getting together—to discuss some form of strategic alliance."

Bud struggled to clear his jet-lagged mind. He wasn't sure he understood what he was hearing. He felt as though he were caught in mental quicksand. "Strategic alliance?" His voice sounded tinny to him, and a long way off.

"That's what I'm proposing."

"Richard, my IQ may be set at room temperature, but I'm about three days short of signing one hell of a big deal with Dolan Laboratories, and you're suggesting a strategic alliance? What in the Sam Hill are you up to now?"

"I'm talking about a merger. I'm talking about IPP merging with Whitecliff."

Bud chuckled, removed his tortoise-shell half-glasses and slipped them into his shirt pocket. "You're pulling my leg."

"Not at all. I'm not *pulling* anything. I'm proposing that you terminate your discussions with Dolan immediately and begin discussions with us and, before you respond, I'd like to remind you that a marriage between our companies would make us the largest pharmaceutical company in the world and, I believe, would add substantial value to both our companies' share prices."

"Whoa! Slow down," Bud said. "The horse is already out of the barn. The Dolan deal is done, all except for some small stuff to give the lawyers something to haggle over. Besides, a deal with you would be too one-sided. You'd swallow us whole. And, Richard, in case you've forgotten, you and I might have a real hard time working together."

"I'm sure we can work around all your issues, Bud. I've thoroughly discussed this with my Board and they're all for it," Richard said, and then added, "And, by the way, so is the Prime Minister."

"The Prime Minister? Ah, for Christ's sake, Richard, what are you doing bringing him into this?"

"I didn't bring him in, he stepped in himself. So what do you say? Can we get together this evening and discuss this in a friendly fashion, for if not—as I've heard you say before—there's more than one way to skin a cat."

Is he threatening a take-over? Bud knew a hostile bid for his company would cost in the neighborhood of seventy billion pounds. He also knew Whitecliff could easily raise the capital. And, while he didn't like being threatened, especially by this man, the prospect of having a chance to lead the largest pharmaceutical company in the world had great appeal to him. Further, if Richard was right, it might be an even better deal for his shareholders than the Dolan deal. He sighed. "Okay, Richard, talk's cheap. When and where would you like to meet?"

"In your office, in five minutes."

"In five minutes? Where in hell are you?"

"Outside, in my car," Richard said.

Bud walked to a rain–streaked window and looked down at a silver Jaguar sedan parked in the brightly lit visitor's area in front of IPP House. A tall man sat in the back, holding a phone. The man folded his frame forward, craned his thin neck to look up at him, and waved a long-fingered hand. He hurried back to his desk, told Richard that he'd meet with him and barked at his secretary through his speakerphone. "Joanne, call security. Tell them we're expecting Richard Beecroft and to send him up. Tell Nigel I need to see him right away. And just for the fun of it, see if anyone's left in the law department. On the double, Jo. Chop chop."

Moments later, Finch-Hatton walked into his office. Before he could speak, Bud said, "Nigel, in a minute, Richard Beecroft's coming up here to discuss our companies merging. His sense of timing's God-awful, but I think he's dead serious."

"I should hope so," Nigel said. "A deal with Whitecliff could do wonders for our share price."

There was a coolness, an aloofness, to Nigel's tone that Bud knew only too well. He stood, stuffed the tail of his white shirt into his gray suit trousers and leaned forward, placing his hands, fingers spread wide, on his desk. He searched Nigel's face for a clue to what his hidden agenda might be this time. "Goddamn it, Nigel, what are you talking about? We've been through all of this before." He felt his temper rising and caught the irritation in his voice. "Whitecliff's so damn much bigger than we are, I can't see any way—no matter what Richard's got up his sleeve—that it could be a merger of equals. In the end, they'll take us over."

"But in this case, they took the initiative. Richard called *us*."

"I don't give a possum's ass who called whom," Bud said. "They're still too damn big for us. Besides, we've struck a sweet deal with Dolan, and if we cut them off and this thing with Whitecliff falls through, we'll be plum out of potential partners. And you and I—yes, *you* and I, Nigel—will be circulating our resumes hoping to find someone dumb enough to hire us. And how in God's name would I ever explain this to David Dolan?"

"It would be rather simple, I would say," Nigel said. "Simply tell him you've received a better offer."

"Simple as that?" Bud shook his head in disgust. "Goddamn, Nigel, I don't think you understand, or I don't understand you. David and I go way back. He's like family to me." He straightened and walked to the window. The interior light of the silver sedan showed only the driver reading a newspaper.

He turned and faced his CFO. "Look, Nigel, I'm putting all my cards on the table. You should know that Richard and I have never gotten along all that well, that at times things get pretty raw between us."

"You can't let your personal biases interfere now," Nigel said. "With your friend Dolan or with Richard."

"You think I just fell off the turnip truck?" Bud said. "I know the rules as well as anyone, but I think we should discuss my relationship with Richard before this goes—"

Nigel glanced toward the glass office wall and held up a hand. "Too late now. He's here."

Bud muttered, "Shoot!" and walked outside his office to meet Richard. "Of course y'all know each other," he said as Beecroft and Finch-Hatton greeted each other formally. "Nigel knows why you're here, Richard, so if you don't mind, I'd like him to join us."

Richard shrugged.

"Also, I want to go on the record that this is nothing more than an exploratory conversation. Are we absolutely clear on that?"

Richard smiled but Bud couldn't tell if he was being polite or mocking him. "Yes, an informal, exploratory chat. That's precisely what this meeting is. Nothing more. No commitments."

"Okay," Bud said. "Let's see what you've got."

Richard sat in one of four low, white leather chairs that surrounded a glass-topped coffee table. He pulled two black binders from his briefcase and placed one in front of Bud and kept the other for himself. *Lazard Brothers* was stenciled in gold in the lower right-hand corner of each binder. "I've asked Lazard to do a bit of homework for this meeting," he said, placing his long hands flat on the black binder in front of him. He paused and gave Haney and Finch-Hatton a thin smile.

Nigel leaned forward and smiled back at him.

The old-boys-club smile. Bud chuckled, pushed his hands into his pants pockets, crossed his feet and stretched his legs. "No offense, Richard, but this is the first 'informal, exploratory chat' I've ever had with an evaluation from an investment banker that's thick enough to choke a horse."

"We engaged Lazard only to make sure it was worth your time to discuss this," Richard said. "They have made some reasonable assumptions and worked up pro-forma statements for our combined business. If you'll turn to page twenty-one, you'll find their projections." He waited for him to find the page. "As you can see, it could be a very powerful deal—a deal The City and Wall Street would heartily endorse." He paused. "It would increase both our companies' values considerably. Take a moment to look it over."

Bud stifled a yawn and slid his book closer to Nigel so his CFO could study the projections, but two of Lazard's major assumptions had already registered with him: a 60/40 merger and dramatic lift in IPP's share price. As Nigel studied the proposal, Bud wondered how he would gracefully terminate his dealings with David Dolan and accept the management structure of 60/40, putting Beecroft and Whitecliff in the driver's seat. He stood and walked to the window. Richard followed him.

"Bud, I need you to help me do this," Richard said. "It's not only the size of the company that's so compelling. This is about new drug discovery. That's what makes this idea so brilliant. What does Dolan have other than lomaxidine?"

"They don't need much else."

"But think of *our* combined research budget; it would be the largest in the industry. We'd be unstoppable."

Bud looked at Richard, and for a moment wondered what it was about this man that made him dislike him so. Was it their history? Or because Richard had proposed a deal that had upset his equilibrium? "You know, no matter how good the numbers are, or how good your deal may be strategically, this puts me in one hell of a fix. And what happens if your proposal falls through? I could end up looking as dumb as a box of rocks."

Richard stared out the window without answering while Nigel continued to pore over the financial projections, apparently oblivious to what was going on around him. Finally, Richard said, "This deal will *not* fall through. You have my word on that. Further, the Prime Minister feels our reaching some kind of agreement is in Britain's best interests. I *know* it's in our companies' best interests. I will do anything—*anything at all*—to see that it does not fail."

"Well, if I have your word on that, Richard, I'll get back to you tomorrow by the close of play."

"Excellent," Richard said, and started toward the door without shaking hands.

"Nigel, if you don't mind, I'd like a word with Richard before he leaves," Bud said.

Nigel stood, said good-bye, and quietly closed the office door behind him.

Bud waited until he felt he had Richard's attention. "Richard, I'm going to be real open with you. There's one thing that you must agree to if I'm going to seriously consider your proposal, because sixty-forty's just too damn lop-sided. What's more, I can't change horses in midstream unless there's something in it for me. So, unless you're prepared to have me as the Chief Executive of the merged company, there's no deal. That may be asking a lot of you, given our history and all, but it's a deal breaker for me."

"I've already given the matter some thought."

"And?"

"It will take some doing, but I think it can be arranged."

"I'm going to need more assurances than just a *think,* Richard, so why don't you *think* on it some more and we'll discuss it tomorrow. But let's get one thing straight right now: if I can't be CEO, there's no deal. You got that? No CEO, no deal. Not now. Not ever."

Richard reached for the large chrome door handle and pulled the heavy glass door open. "I'll wait for your call," he said, and then added, "I hope we can do this amicably." He stepped through the door, raised the tip of his index finger above his eyebrow to signal good-bye.

Bud shook his head and reached for his speakerphone. "Jo, get me JJ on the phone please, and try to find Sir Christopher. And call Alfredo. I'd like to have dinner at Chester Square with JJ and Chris and Nigel. Let's shoot for eight-thirty."

A moment later, his phone buzzed. "It's Miss Jennings," his secretary said.

He picked up. "JJ, I hope you don't have something planned for this evening, because if you do, I'm afraid I'm going to have to ask you to cancel it. Something's come up that we *must* discuss."

"Has something gone wrong with DIP?"

"Nah, everything's just dandy with the Dolan folks. I need your help with a horse of a different color."

JJ laughed. "What in the world are you talking about?"

"I need to talk to you and Nigel and Chris, and I don't want to discuss it over the phone."

"Nigel and Chris will be there? So much for a nice quiet dinner." She paused. "Sorry," she said, and lowered her voice in a way that made Bud think she sounded a bit hurt. "It's just hard to know how businesslike the situation is when your client is talking about horses of a different color."

"You'll find out soon enough."

He hung up and sat at his desk; the lights in his office and over his secretary's work station the only ones, other than those for security, still burning in IPP's headquarters. Through the glass wall, he watched as his secretary pulled on her raincoat and collected her umbrella. She pushed his office door half open and leaned in. "I located Sir Christopher. He'll be at Chester Square as close to eight-thirty as he can make it. Do you need me for anything else?"

"That's it for tonight, Jo. But if you can, I'd appreciate it if you'd get in a shade early tomorrow."

"Never a dull moment," she said and, with a smile, waved goodnight.

"Never a dull moment," he muttered to himself, and wondered what kind of a fix he was getting himself into and what a nice, quiet dinner alone with JJ would be like.

CHAPTER 6

Anxious—for one reason in particular—to learn how Richard Beecroft's proposal would be received, Nigel Finch-Hatton was first to arrive at the IPP property on Chester Square where he was ushered to a sitting room by the butler, poured a glass of wine and left to his thoughts. He paced the room for a moment and then sat in a gold-and-ochre-upholstered Queen Anne chair, the heels of his black shoes and his dark-trousered knees locked together like those of a schoolboy posing for his class picture. He combed the few remaining strands of gray hair over his prominently arched bald spot with his fingers, drew the Lazard Frères evaluation from his briefcase and placed it on his lap. He let it sit, unopened, even though he was excited by what Lazard's projections could mean to him for in the last few years he had lost a large portion of his fortune through the Lloyd's of London investment scandal and, as a result, constantly worried about his future and his ability to retain his country home and maintain a lifestyle he thought fitting for a man of his station. For the first time in his life his job had become a financial necessity, a fact that was distasteful to him. Like so many of his public school friends, he held the actual managing of the day-to-day business in low regard, dismissing it privately as the work of men like Bud Haney—"the commercial operators." In his view, it was not a gentleman's pastime; that distinction fell to lawyers, doctors, some civil servants, the clergy and the military. But, while Nigel looked down his nose at Haney and "his American country-boy demeanor," he knew he could ill afford to fall out of favor with him, for he now relied heavily on his salary and his bonus that most years brought his total annual compensation close to £1,000,000.

This evening—although he had been a strong supporter of the Dolan deal because of its impact on his personal wealth—he was prepared to shift his support and allegiance to Beecroft and Whitecliff. He had set a target of five million pounds in profit from his IPP stock options before retiring and was hopeful that if the Whitecliff deal became a reality, his goal would soon be reached. With these thoughts, Nigel took a sip of his wine and stroked the Lazard binder somewhat lovingly.

Bud arrived next and joined Nigel in the sitting room. The prospect of becoming Chief Executive of the most powerful company in his industry—the lead dog—filled his thoughts. Alfredo poured him a lager and led Nigel and him to the dining room. When they were seated, Bud told him that Chris Pearson and JJ were on their way.

"You needed her for this?"

"You got a problem with that?" Bud said.

"In a way, yes. Chris and you and I could have handled this without her."

"She's a good sounding board and we may need her to do some analysis. You're not unhappy with her work, are you?"

Nigel shook his head. "No, but . . ."

"But what?"

"She's more involved in our business than I would like."

"Nigel, this is a discussion for another time. Right now, I'm concerned about Beecroft's proposal, not to mention—" Bud stopped as JJ pushed through the dining room door and hustled to the table. As always not a hair was out of place but—as meticulous as she was in her appearance—somehow, unlike the polished London School of Economics-, Harvard- and Wharton-educated men who worked for her, she frequently seemed to be running late, to have forgotten something, to have encountered a catastrophe somewhere along the line.

"Sorry I'm late," she said. "There's a 'do' of some kind going on at Mrs. Thatcher's and I had to park blocks away."

Bud stood and pulled a chair from the table for her. She set a narrow black leather briefcase on the floor and settled her thin figure in the chair, then shifted closer to the table, knocking over an empty crystal goblet. "Sorry," she said, as she righted the glass. She looked across the table and smiled. "Well, hi, Nigel."

Nigel nodded.

JJ told Alfredo she'd like a glass of pinot grigio and turned to Bud and asked what horse of a different color they were there to discuss; asked if there was a problem.

"Not a problem," Nigel said. "An opportunity."

"More like a little of both," Bud said.

As she began to ask again what was going on, the door opened and Sir Christopher Pearson, chairman of three of Britain's leading companies—Blue Oval Industries, Stokeware China and, most notably, IPP—strutted into the dining room, his shoulders squared, his double-breasted Prince of Wales check suit buttoned across his flat stomach, his wiry black hair combed back across the tops of his elephantine ears.

"Gentlemen, JJ, sorry I'm late. Maggie seems to be entertaining tonight and the traffic is bloody awful." He seated himself quickly between Bud and Nigel and watched as wine was poured for him. "Cheers, all," he said, raising his glass to each, his large brown eyes fixing Finch-Hatton and then Haney from beneath sharply arched black eyebrows. "Very well, Bud, what's the urgent topic? I certainly hope nothing untoward has happened with Dolan."

"All's well with Dolan," Bud said, and then took his boss through the events of earlier that evening.

"You're not serious," JJ said. She looked at Nigel, who nodded, and she waved her hands in front of her, signaling for all to disregard her comment. "He's serious. Sorry."

Bud drew the Lazard Brothers binder from his briefcase and handed it to JJ. "Richard left this behind. He and the folks at Lazard think The City and Wall Street will love the deal. They think it could add another fifteen percent to our share price."

"Nigel, do you agree?" Chris said.

Nigel beamed. "Perhaps even more."

"Interesting," Chris said.

"That's it," Bud said. "Except for one other thing; I told Richard that if we were to accept his proposal, I must be the CEO. Otherwise, it would be an outright take-over and they'd swallow us whole."

Before Chris could respond, Nigel said, "We can't let our personal goals stand in the way of what's best for our shareholders."

Bud reddened and started to say something but was cut off by his chairman. "Of course you're right, Nigel, but I don't think that's the case here. On the contrary, I think Bud makes an excellent point: the management structure and who controls the company are inseparable, and must be decided early on."

"Okay, JJ, I guess that's it," Bud said. "We'll get together tomorrow to see what you and your people come up with."

"Tomorrow, it is," JJ said, struggling to find room in her

briefcase for the Lazard binder. "I do have a couple of questions—concerns, actually—before I excuse myself."

"Fire away," Bud said.

JJ adjusted the silverware by her empty plate. "This means you'd work for Richard Beecroft, right?"

"Is that really material?" Chris asked.

"Maybe not material," Bud said, "but it's something worth thinking about. Richard and I have a bit of history. There were a bunch of years there when we weren't on the best of terms; more accurately, when we didn't speak."

"And what, pray tell, was this history about?" Chris said.

Bud said it was water over the dam and not worth talking about.

"Well, I'd like to know," Chris said. "After all, it was you who said working for Richard was something worth thinking about, and you know as well as I do that things like 'history' can derail the best of business negotiations."

Bud sighed. "It's not that big a deal, really, Chris. Years ago when Richard was running Whitecliff's US operations, Dolan and Whitecliff got all tangled up in a lawsuit and it became the talk of the industry. The Wall Street Journal and The Pink Sheet just couldn't let it go—David sues Goliath, stuff like that. Well, a couple of months later we're all—Arch and David and me—we're at the PMA annual meeting, when Richard says he's got a story we've all just got to hear." He took a sip of his lager, noted that Chris' face showed no expression and worried that his English chairman might not understand the significance of the story, but felt there was no turning back. "Well, the next thing you know, Richard tells this long damn joke in front of everybody that ends up calling Dolan Laboratories a Mickey Mouse outfit."

Nigel smiled almost gleefully, Bud thought. JJ adjusted her silverware again. Chris Pearson remained expressionless.

"Well, we won the lawsuit. Won the Mickey Mouse War, as it was called throughout the industry—and the day the court finding was announced, every representative of the company who called on a doctor or a pharmacist wore a Mickey Mouse tie or a Mickey Mouse scarf and introduced themselves as being from that 'Mickey Mouse outfit, Dolan Laboratories, who just beat Whitecliff in a court of law.' As you might imagine, it pissed old Richard off something fierce."

Chris chuckled. "All good stuff, but I'm sure enough time has passed that you and Richard can work things out."

"I hope so, Chris, but you must understand one thing. It was Beecroft who took it to the gutter, not Dolan Laboratories. It was Richard who was breaking the law."

"Bud, I do understand, but you can't let it get in the way of Beecroft's proposal," Chris said. "There's too much at stake here." He leaned toward JJ. "You said you had two questions."

JJ looked at Bud like a child hoping for permission to speak. He nodded at her. She adjusted her silver setting yet again. "I wouldn't be doing my job if I didn't ask about the deal with Dolan and how—"

"Let's not worry about Dolan for now," Chris interrupted. "If the deal with Whitecliff is in our shareholders' best interests, we'll cross the Dolan bridge when we have to. After all, there isn't anyone better equipped to handle the Dolan family than Bud." He nodded as though he were pleased with his response. "Does that answer your question?"

"Partially," JJ said, "but I think you should give how and when you cut Dolan off a lot of thought."

Chris sat back in his chair and folded his arms across his chest. "This is big business, JJ. All of us at this table are paid to make the hard decisions, even if they're personally painful."

JJ's face colored slightly. "That fact hasn't escaped me," she said. At that moment, Bud thought there was an uncharacteristic chill to both JJ and Chris' tones and it occurred to him that Beecroft's visit had raised the stakes and the complexity of all their jobs; had increased the pressure and the anxiety level for everyone, including him. He wondered if the stakes were just as high, and the pressure just as great, for his old nemesis when JJ said, "I also think you should give an equal amount of thought to how you obtain Dr. Beecroft's assurances that this deal will go through. You pay GilbertBeard a lot of money for our advice, and I'd be delinquent if I didn't raise that as an issue."

Chris kept his arms crossed and rolled his shoulders forward. "And exactly what is the issue?"

JJ never shifted her eyes from his. "It's the first law of wing walking, Chris: never let go of one thing until you've got something else firmly in hand." Before Chris could respond, she stood and looked at Bud as though she may have just made a career-ending comment. "Well, I wasn't all that hungry anyway. What time would you like us at IPP House?"

"Can y'all be there by ten?" Bud said.

"Ten it is," she answered, and excused herself.

Bud watched her leave the room, and felt a sudden emptiness as she closed the door. As always, she's hit the nail square on the head.

CHAPTER 7

The digital message on the gray leather bulkhead in front of Bud Haney read: MACH 2.00; FEET 55500, while on the right-hand bulkhead the display recorded: TEMP -60°C; MPH 1340. Bud yawned and leaned across the empty window seat and looked through the small oval at the brightening sky. The Concorde was almost two hours into its flight across the Atlantic and the sun had begun to glow again as the plane approached the coastline of Canada. He placed his hand on the window and felt its warmth, the warmth created by rocketing through the sub-zero air at twice the speed of sound. As always, he thought it an odd sensation to be traveling at Mach 2 and not be able to see the swept-back wings that carried him and, for an instant, remembered how difficult it was to see the wings of his A-4 Skyhawk, then imagined the right wing shredding and tearing away and heard his call of "Mayday! Mayday! I'm hit!" He shuddered as though a chill had run through him and took off his watch to set it to US time. He had left London at seven in the evening and would arrive in

New York a few minutes before six. He moved the dial on his watch back five hours and noted that it was a little after four in Princeton or wherever David Dolan might be at that moment.

He pushed his seat back and placed a small white pillow behind his head, thinking that he would unwind a little—that the issues he was dealing with were too weighty, too numerous, to let him sleep. *As they should be,* he thought, for he was making pharmaceutical history with this merger. *And nobody ever said it would be easy.* He turned his head toward the window, closed his eyes, and his thoughts turned to the day's events. He was satisfied that his role had been clarified, even though it had been difficult to get a commitment from Richard. "Just give me a simple yes, or no," he had said. "Am I the CEO or not?" And Richard asked if it was a requirement of his Board. "I'll take care of my Board, you take care of yours," he answered angrily. "Do we have an agreement or don't we?" And finally, when Richard said they had an agreement, he thought, *Well, I'll be goddamned—the lead dog of the most powerful company in* my *industry. Not too shabby for an orphan boy from Hope Hull.* He smiled and gave in to the warmth of the cabin and fatigue.

In his sleep he drifted back to the morning's meeting and saw David Dolan in a large four-poster double bed in the corner of his boardroom, lying beside his college sweetheart and wife of twenty-three years, occasionally brushing her with his hand, sleeping heavily, knowing that he had done the right thing for his family's business, secure in the fact that he was turning it over to the one man in the industry he could count on, and Bud woke and called David's name out loud and then sat upright and glanced across the aisle to see if he was being watched, but his fellow passengers were busy organizing themselves for landing as the sign on the bulkheads read *Thank You For Flying Concorde.*

He patted his cheeks to wake himself more fully, buttoned his collar and drew the knot of his tie in place. He steeled himself for what he was about to do and thought of what JJ had said. Was he letting go of a good thing with nothing more than a promise from a lifelong enemy that he had something better firmly in hand?

The black Lincoln Town Car delivered him to the Four Seasons Hotel at ten minutes past seven. He checked in quickly, took the elevator to the fourth floor and hurried down the deep, beige-carpeted hallway. He pushed the bell for 4612 and looked at his watch. *Almost twelve-thirty in London.* He was tired and hungry. He drew a deep breath and readied himself.

When David opened the door the two men raised their right hands and clasped them firmly together and held tight for a moment. "You must be shot," David said.

Bud thought there was a tentative air to his voice. "I'll be better when I've had something to drink."

"Well, you've come to the right place," David said, and limped to the small bar in the corner of the suite and poured a beer for Bud and scotch on the rocks for himself.

Bud slipped off his suit jacket and folded it over the back of an overstuffed chair and the two men sat opposite one another and raised their glasses. "Here's to you," David said. "And to DIP."

"To good friends," Bud said, forcing a smile.

For a few seconds neither spoke.

"How's the recall going?" Bud asked.

"It is what it is: one hell of a lot of work and a real pain in the ass."

"And your dad?"

"Another pain in the ass. He hasn't spoken more than two words to me since we voted to do the deal."

"Is he pissed at me?" Bud said.

"No. He only blames me and . . ."

"And what?"

David looked at the floor. "He keeps saying my brother wouldn't have sold out on him."

"But Arch never . . ." He stopped himself. "I'm sorry, David. Real sorry."

"It's okay; it's not the first time." David raised his eyes to meet Bud's. "So, what's up? Is there a problem with the deal?"

David's abrupt change of subject caught Bud off guard and he squinted at him as though he were trying to see things more clearly. *His father's doing a number on him and now I'm about to do the same.* "Well, yes, but it's not a personal thing. Let's get that straight, right from the start."

David straightened his right leg and massaged his thigh with both hands. "You're going to ask me to get out of the way once we've signed the agreement."

"No, David; nothing like that." He tried to buy himself a little time. "I swear," he said. He leaned forward in his chair and cupped his hands around his beer glass; drew a deep breath. "I said it was nothing personal, and I meant it." He hesitated again. "I don't know quite how to tell you this, old friend, but our deal's off."

"Off?"

Bud nodded.

"You've got to be kidding!"

"I'm afraid not," he said in a voice close to a whisper.

"What are you talking about? The one man I thought I could trust and you've betrayed me?"

"David, David, David," Bud said, raising his hands in surrender. "I didn't betray *you*. Please. It's a business decision, pure and simple. We've been approached—"

"I don't care what happened. You've gone back on your word," David yelled. "You've ruined me. Me *and* my family. Totally screwed me with my father and hung my company out to dry. I'll say it again, Bud: you—of all people—have betrayed me."

Bud could feel his face beginning to flush. "David, listen for a moment. Betrayal's a bit strong, don't you think? I mean, is that what you called it when you decided to sell your family's business? Your father called it 'selling out,' but I remember you saying it was something else. I remember you calling it a business decision."

"It's not the same thing, and you know it," David said. "Our company will be in play the minute this news hits the street, and any hope of getting things back on track with Dad are gone. And after all I've done to try to get him . . ." David shook his head, and smiled a smile of disgust. "What the hell *did* happen?"

"You want the whole story or just the executive summary?"

"Every ugly detail," David said, kneading his thigh. "I'll need them all for Dad . . . and more."

Bud recounted the sequence of events with great precision. "So, in the end, it came down to which deal was better for our shareholders. All agreed Whitecliff was the way to go."

"*All* agreed?"

He nodded. "Me included."

"How could you do it? And with that Mickey Mouse son of a bitch Beecroft of all people. He tried to screw our family and he'll try to screw you. Mark my words."

"I feel kind of funny telling you this, being my friend and all," Bud said, "but the answer is simple: shareholder value."

"Well, fuck shareholder value and fuck you being my friend. The Bud Haney I used to know was a bigger man than you are today. Remember our agreement to tell the other when he's getting off track? Remember those long talks about the role honesty and trust play in a friendship? In business? Well, you've sold out, Bud. Sold out your principles, and, now, sold out your friends."

"The Bud Haney you used to know wasn't a CEO with shareholders crawling in his shorts."

"Easy for you to say but how do I make sense of this to my father? You've made me look like a fool with my family. You've ruined everything."

"David, please," Bud said. "I've always stood by my word, and by you. Don't forget, I cut your father off when he approached me—"

"Approached you?"

He looked at David and nodded.

David yelled it this time. "Approached you? What the hell are you talking about?"

Bud slowly shook his head. "Ah, God damn, David, I've messed this up but good. Let's call it quits right now and get you and me back on track."

"Dad offered you my job, didn't he?"

He avoided David's watery blue stare.

"Well, didn't he?"

Bud sighed. "I thought you knew. I thought somewhere along the line he'd have told you. But he never really offered me the job, we just talked about it, and I cut him off."

"First my father betrays me, then my friend. This is a great goddamn business I've gotten myself into."

"David, I'll say it again. I didn't betray you and neither did your father. He was just doing his homework and I'm sure today he thinks he picked the best man."

"Right. Other than my brother and you." David took a long drink of his scotch. "I've heard enough. You've done your duty; delivered your message. Now, get out of here."

Bud stood, pulled on his jacket, moved in front of David and put out his hand. "Believe me, I'm real sorry it ended this way; that I added insult to injury. I wanted so badly to do this right."

"Bullshit! I'll never believe another thing you tell me." David stood, brushed past

his outstretched hand and limped toward the bar. "Go on, get out."

Bud walked to the door, opened it and turned to David. His words came slowly. "I'm real sorry. Maybe someday I'll be able to prove it to you. Our friendship means the world to me." He buttoned his jacket and slid his hands in the pockets, waiting for his friend to face him, to say something. David gave him a sharp look of disdain but said nothing. He shrugged. "Well, I wish you and your family the very best in everything. I mean it. The *very* best. Y'all take good care."

He waited another moment in silence, and then closed the door quietly behind him.

Bud ordered a hamburger and a beer through room service, and called JJ. Her voice was husky with sleep when she answered.

"Hey, it's me," he said. "Sorry to call you so late but I thought I'd check in."

"I was hoping you'd call. How'd it go?"

He didn't answer.

"Bud? Are you there? How'd he take it?"

His voice broke as he told her it was a goddamn nightmare. "I told him it was a business decision; he called it betrayal."

"But he must understand that lots of times they're one and the same," JJ said.

"But he's spent so much emotional capital with his father to get this deal done, and now I've gone and pulled the rug out from under him without any goddamned warning."

"But things are moving so fast, you didn't have time to warn him."

"But he needed this deal so much more than I did. It was do or die for him and I screwed him."

"Give it some time," JJ said.

For a moment neither spoke. Finally, Bud said, "JJ, friends don't grow on trees and I just lost a real good one."

"I'm sorry, but deep down he's got to know how difficult this was for you."

"I'm not so sure. He says I've changed. Says I've sold out, and I'm afraid he may be right. Maybe my ego's getting as big as all the rest."

"Nonsense. He said that in the heat of the moment. When he cools down, he'll realize that it wasn't anything personal—that it was your job. Of all people, he knows the kind of man you are," she said. "And always will be. Now, get some sleep and we'll talk tomorrow night when you get home."

"You're not too bad for a banker," he said.

"It's a service business. Remember?" JJ said, and as he hung up the phone, he heard her add, "Sweet dreams, Buddy. Everything's going to be okay."

CHAPTER 8

"What does he want now?" Arch Dolan stood by the small kitchen table at Fox Hill shaking the remains of a box of Wheaties into his cereal bowl. "Has he got more problems with the FDA?"

"He didn't say, but he sounded very down," Elizabeth answered. She took off her glasses and wiped them clean with her napkin. "Whatever it is, dear, I hope you'll be supportive."

"Supportive?" Arch shoved a milk carton in the refrigerator and slammed the door shut. He turned and stared at her. "How can I be supportive if I don't agree with what he's doing?"

She put her glasses back on and looked at him without her usual warm smile. "There are times you've got to give a little. To let go. You've had your turn. Now it's David's, and he's going to do it differently than you." She smiled briefly. "Please, dear, support him and let him do his job."

"But I didn't agree to sell the business. Remember? You did. You and Ben and Sarah and . . . and for the wrong reason to boot." He rubbed his fingers quickly back and forth across his thumb. "For money, nothing but money."

"That's not fair and you know it," Elizabeth said. "I was trying to do what I thought was right; trying to save your relationship with your son. What possibly could be wrong with that?"

Arch lowered himself into the chair opposite her. "Because it should have been a business decision, not a family one."

"But, Arch, you've said so many times this was about family, so promise me you'll support him and help him when he asks for it."

For a moment he didn't answer. Finally he nodded and said, "If that's what you want, that's what I'll do."

"Good. It's what's best. You'll see." She closed her eyes and massaged her temples with her fingers. "Besides, this whole thing's giving me a splitting headache."

Once again, David decided to deliver the bad news to his father first, but this time he had included his mother, who now played such an unexpectedly important role, hoping that her presence would soften things a bit. Then he would call his Uncle Ben, his Aunt Sarah, and Mike McPartland at the Morgan Bank, it being imperative that he reach all of them before noon when Whitecliff's and IPP's press releases reached the wire services in the US.

Even with his mother present, David was prepared for a long discourse from his father on how this new development proved that the decision to sell the company was the wrong decision, and steeled himself for a lot of what-are-you-going-to-do-nows? And, in the back of his mind, he hoped to find a moment alone with his father to confront him with Bud Haney's other heartbreaking piece of news, one that once again signaled that he was Dolan Laboratories' CEO by default. As he approached the drive to Fox Hill he could hear Susan's advice: *You're the boss now, not your dad, not Bud Haney. You've often said lots of companies would be interested in doing a deal with you, so go find one.* For a moment he smiled, thinking Susan had always been such a positive force, but then shuddered at her parting words—*things could be worse*—because he couldn't possibly imagine how. He swung his Porsche into the wooded drive and was startled by the deafening, metallic bark of a siren and a spinning red light in his rearview mirror. At first he thought his mind had been somewhere else, that he must have been speeding. *Shit! It's not my day,* he thought, but when he studied the vehicle behind him, the word **AMBULANCE**, written in navy blue letters across its white hood, registered with him and instinctively he gunned the Porsche through the wooded portion of the drive, over the loosely slatted, rumbling bridge, then wrenched the steering wheel to the right, forcing the car between two whitewashed stones onto the drive's grassy shoulder. He waited for the ambulance, and then another, to pass and accelerated back onto the gravel and followed them as they sped toward his parents' house. He tried to make sense of the turquoise and white writing in front of him: **LIFE 7—EMERGENCY SERVICES—Lifemobile**.

"Lifemobile?" he said aloud. "Dad? What the hell is going on?"

He braked just short of the ambulances and struggled free from his seat belt and pulled his right thigh beneath the steering wheel. As he climbed from his car, EMTs and paramedics were wrestling equipment from the backs of their vehicles and a voice was cackling tinnily over their radio, its squelch seeming to interrupt every word. No one acknowledged him as they quickly and efficiently went about their assigned routines.

"What's going on?" he said.

One of the emergency crew slammed the doors shut at the back of his ambulance and asked, "Is this the front door?"

"Yes," David yelled, "but what the hell's going on?"

"Where's the kitchen?"

"The kitchen?" He hesitated. "Down the hall to the left. I'll show you. Won't someone please tell me what's going on?"

"We're responding to a 911," the EMT said. "A Mr. Dolan called about his wife."

David gasped a breath of cold air. "His wife?" *I don't believe it.* He pushed by the paramedics, ran to the front door, and opened it. "Dad? Dad? Where are you?"

He heard his father call from the kitchen. "Son, come quick."

The uniformed men followed David as he ran toward his father's voice. All stopped at the kitchen door. Elizabeth lay on the floor, gray-skinned, staring blankly at the ceiling. There was a small patch of blood near the crown of her wavy white hair. Her glasses sat upright and open on the terra cotta kitchen tiles. David thought they looked like they were searching for something, maybe even him. An overturned chair lay beside her. Her left side was motionless, her right arm and leg shifting back and forth as though she were trying to send a message. Her khaki slacks were dark with urine at the crotch. His father knelt beside her, dabbing the blood in her hair with a paper napkin, muttering, "Elizabeth, please stay with me. Please."

"Dad, what happened?"

His father looked up, his watery blue eyes at once showing fear and fatigue. "We were talking about your visit and the next thing I knew she complained about a headache and in an instant fell off her chair." He glanced at the paramedics who were moving quickly to place a litter next to Elizabeth. "Please save her. She's all I've got left."

David knelt and stroked his mother's cheek, drawing his fingers slowly over her clammy skin. "Hang on, Mom. For God's sake, hang on."

Arch gently touched the napkin to the bloody spot in Elizabeth's hair again and David covered his father's hand with his, and held it still. His father gave him a curious look.

"What next?" David whispered.

The doctor at Princeton Hospital placed her hands on the knees of her sharply creased black slacks and moved her white-sneakered feet together. Her stethoscope swayed in front of her white coat as she leaned forward. "Mr. Dolan?"

Arch waved a hand.

"I'm Dr. Cravello. I'm afraid your wife's suffered a stroke. It appears as though she's experienced a cerebral hemorrhage. She's in a critical state right now." She looked at David as though she were about to ask a question.

"He understands," David said.

The doctor nodded and looked back at Arch. "Mr. Dolan, more than likely an aneurysm—a weak spot in an artery wall—has burst, causing bleeding in the brain. The amount of bleeding determines the severity of the stroke. It's a very serious condition."

"How serious?" Arch said. "And don't give me any medical mumbo jumbo or sugar coating."

"I understand, sir," the doctor said. "Half the time, people who experience a cerebral hemorrhage die from increased pressure on their brains."

The muscles in Arch's jaw began to show and disappear, show and disappear. David reached for his father's arm. Arch pulled David's hand tight against his side. "Is she going to die?" he asked.

"Right now she's on a life-support system—"

"Yes or no," Arch said.

The doctor searched Arch's face. From her look, David already knew her answer. "Yes, sir." She paused. "It's only a matter of when."

"Are you sure?" David asked.

"Yes. We're keeping her alive until you've had a chance to discuss what you want to do."

"What we want to do?" Arch whispered. "My son and I would like to say good-bye to her. That's what we'd like to do. After that, I only ask that she go peacefully."

"There's no rush to decide, Mr. Dolan," Dr. Cravello said. "It's a very difficult decision, and it's come upon you so unexpectedly."

"We've talked about this many times, and I know what she wants," Arch said. "All I ask is that I'm holding her when she leaves me."

The doctor straightened and slipped her hands into the pockets of her coat. "You'll be holding her, sir. I can promise you that."

Arch stood slowly, drawing David with him, still holding David's hand between his arm and his side. "Come on, son. Let's go say good-bye to your mother."

The business struggles that had consumed David and kept him awake the night before had evaporated. He no longer cared that his best chance to save the company had gone down the drain, that his father had no confidence in him, that his best friend had betrayed him. At this moment all he wanted was to shield his mother from anything that might frighten her, that might cause her pain. And he wanted to support and be close to his father, to begin to get things back on the right track. He tightened his grip on the old man's arm, and the two of them followed the doctor without speaking through the entrance to *Triage 1,* shoulder to shoulder, their pale blue eyes glistening with tears and fixed straight ahead.

"This car was designed for a younger man," Arch said as he ducked his head and lowered himself into the bucket seat of David's Porsche.

"I'm beginning to think you're right." David started the car and pulled away from the hospital's emergency parking lot. "Getting in and out of it gets harder every day. I'm thinking of trading it in."

"Nonsense. You love it, and you know it." Arch pulled his seatbelt across his chest and locked it in place. "It always reminds your mother of how you liked to go fast in everything when you were a boy."

"I always thought Mom hated it."

"No, David." Arch cleared his throat. "She loves—loved—everything about you."

His father's words surrounded him like an embrace, but he knew that he had to put this and his mother's death aside for a moment. He knew he had to tell his father about his meeting with Bud Haney before the business reporters began to call. He checked the luminous orange numbers on the digital clock, **10:55,** and drew a deep breath. "Dad, listen up for a minute." He opened and closed his hands on the steering wheel. "I know my timing's lousy, but I've got something I need to tell you before we get home."

"More problems with the company?" his father said.

"Yes. More problems."

"It can't be any worse than what we've just been through."

"You're right, but from a business standpoint it's . . ." David hesitated. "It's a surprise, to say the least. You're not going to believe this, but last night Bud called off our deal." He kneaded his thigh and waited.

Silence.

"I was on my way over this morning to tell you."

His father still didn't say a word. David turned to him. "Dad, are you okay? Do you understand what I'm telling you?"

Arch looked out the window on his side of the car, turning his head, appearing to read each road sign they passed as though he was looking for one that would show him the way home, and suddenly it occurred to David that, as a result of his mother's death, his father was back in control of their company, and he wondered if he were considering vetoing his plan and taking charge again, but he didn't think this was either the time or the place to ask. Finally, his father said, "Yes, I'm all right, and of course I understand what you're saying. What happened?"

David thought he sounded as though he were almost feigning interest to be polite, but knew he must keep him focused for a minute more. "Bud got a better offer at the last minute and changed his mind. He betrayed us, Dad."

He waited for the lecture on the wrongness of the original decision—for the what-are-you-going-to-do-nows?—but his father simply raised his large-knuckled left hand and tapped the dash. "It's a setback, but it's not something we have to deal with today."

David felt a great sense of relief, but feared it might be temporary. "I agree, but I had to tell you because it becomes public knowledge at noon. Do you understand? I don't want you to think that this is in any way as important as what just happened." Out of the corner of his eye he saw his father nod. "And, frankly, Dad, I still can't believe that Bud would do this to me. Not only to me, but to you, too. To all of us. I thought he was my friend. I thought he was a friend of the family."

"It's all part of the game," Arch said. He sounded tired and resigned. Defeated. "It wasn't really an act of treachery. It was just business, that's all." At first David couldn't believe that his father would make excuses for Bud's behavior. *But of course it makes sense. Isn't he the man he really wanted to run his company?* "Enough of business," Arch continued. "We've had enough bad news for one day. Besides, I don't have the stomach for it anymore. With your mother gone, it seems as though I don't have anything left. It's over now. The company's yours and I'm near the end of the road and all of a sudden I don't know where I belong."

"You belong with me. And Susan. And the girls," David said. "And, please, Dad, let's not have business come between us ever again. Life's too—"

"Too short?" Arch laughed. "Right now it seems like it's too damned long." He rubbed his hands together as though he were warming them and whispered, "I always thought I'd go first." He turned away from David and looked out the window and slapped his hands on his thighs. "No more. It's too much for me."

David drove slowly along the drive to Fox Hill. He imagined the siren and the flashing light behind him and heard the words, "A Mr. Dolan called about his wife." He parked the car and sat in silence with his father, both staring blankly through the windshield. David was the first to speak. "Susan and the girls are going to be heartbroken. I don't quite know how to tell them. We all loved Mom so much. And Dad, I'm sorry about the way things have turned out. I'd like to put all that behind us."

Arch unbuckled his seat belt and sighed, "Time heals all wounds."

David hoped he was right, that time would heal *their* wounds. He waited for him to say more; watched as he silently reached for the door handle, struggled to get up from the low-slung seat and shuffled toward the house. He followed him, stopping to salute the flag that drooped lifeless at half-mast. *It's been one hell of a day, big brother. One hell of a day.*

He hurried to the front door, pushed it open and waited for his father to go ahead of him, thinking that within the past twelve hours he'd lost his mother and a great friend and an good opportunity to right his family's business. And, now, as he entered the Dolan homestead that suddenly felt so cold and empty, he prepared himself to call his aunt and uncle to give them the shocking news, not only about their sister-in-law, but about their company, too.

CHAPTER 9

As he finished dressing, Richard glanced at the recently in-stalled Jacuzzi with its smooth porcelain curves and stainless fixtures and the thought of the sexual gymnastics that Fiona and he had performed there the night before caused him to smile. He took one last look at her through the bedroom door, asleep, her naked shoulders showing above a thick, down-filled duvet. Intent upon not waking her, he switched off the light and crept down the carpeted stairs, holding his briefcase tightly in his left hand and wincing at every step that creaked beneath him.

At the bottom of the stairs he noted that the morning papers had yet to be delivered. It pleased him for it meant that he was on his schedule, or even a bit ahead. "Good," he said to himself. "I'll be at my desk by seven." He looked through his large front window at sheets of wind-driven rain that glistened past the streetlights lining Alexander Terrace, the "proper" ad-dress where he and Fiona had moved the day after they re-turned from their honeymoon. He selected a black raincoat from a hook in the entrance hall, buttoned it to his throat, belted it tightly at his waist, and slipped out the front door and hurried to the silver Jaguar sedan that waited for him.

"Enjoying this weather, Dr. Beecroft?" his driver asked.

Richard saw the man's dark eyes look to him in the rear-view mirror. He placed his briefcase between his feet and, without looking up, said, "No matter. Not much I can do about it anyhow." As he spoke, his attention was drawn to a stack of newspapers on the seat next to him. "Now, if you wouldn't mind," he said, "I have some urgent reading to do this morning."

"I think you'll find it interesting, sir," his driver said.

Richard lifted the first paper, the European edition of *The Wall Street Journal,* and spread it across his lap. In the upper right-hand corner of the front page the headline read: **<u>Genetic Giant</u> Whitecliff and IPP To Merge—Cost Of Drug Research Is Driving Talks—New Colossus Could Afford Molecular Engineering Needed To Stay On Top.**

Good. All the right buttons pushed. He circled the headline with his index finger several times. *Drug Research. Molecular Engineering. Staying on top.* "Excellent!" he said aloud, then nodded at his driver who glanced at him in the mirror. He read the article carefully. *All business. And all good. Only one oblique reference to potential job losses.* He smiled. *That should please Benson and the Prime Minister.*

He laid *The Financial Times* on top of *The Wall Street Journal.* Its headline read: **Whitecliff and IPP in merger discussions—Drug discovery, combined sales of £28.5 billion and synergies cited as rationale.** The article that followed was analytical and straightforward. *They should be thrilled at 10 Downing Street! I've done everything they asked, and more.* He ran a hand across the salmon-colored paper and nodded. *Nothing to worry about. Benson has kept his word. Fiona will be delighted!* And, for an instant, he imagined himself being called forward by The Lord Chamberlain and kneeling before The Queen in the ballroom at Buckingham Palace, Her Majesty smiling down upon him and saying, "Well done, Sir Richard, you've kept British pharma on British soil." And he would respond, "My duty, Ma'am," before bowing as she raised her sword and tapped him on each shoulder and then slipped the ribbon that held the cross of the Knights Bachelor over his head and let the decoration drop silently against his pounding chest.

He glanced at *The Guardian,* the next paper on the pile: **Whitecliff Sabotages IPP Acquisition—Two Giants To Merge—15,000 Jobs On The Block.**

"Damn it!" he mumbled as he grabbed for the paper, crumpling its edges in his grip. *Jobs on the block! Where did the figure of 15,000 come from? Another leak in my company? No help from the PM's office there.* He began to skim the article, searching for the reference to job losses, telling himself that they would have to appear sooner or later, when, out of the corner of his eye, he caught the headline of the remaining paper, *The Galaxy.* **HOME WRECKING AGAIN! Whitecliff Drug Lord Richard Beecroft Seduces IPP At Eleventh Hour Stranding Dolan Labs At The Altar.**

His heart began to race and he felt a shortness of breath. "Pull over," he barked at his driver. "No, not here. Keep going. I'll tell you what to do." He stared at the headline in *The Galaxy* and then glanced again at *The Guardian,* then back to *The Galaxy*. He found it increasingly difficult to breathe. Sweat trickled from his temples down his cheeks and his neck. He pushed the small chrome lever to lower his window. The cold November air rushed by him, cooling him slightly, ruffling the edges of the newspapers. Rain sprayed through the opening. He slammed his hands, fingers spread wide, on top of the papers to hold them in place. "Damn it!" he said, and closed the window. He saw his driver look at him again but quickly look away. He forced himself to draw deep breaths. He placed *The Galaxy* in front of him and stared at **HOME WRECK-ING AGAIN!** He reached in the pocket of his dark suit jacket, pulled out a neatly folded white handkerchief and wiped his forehead and cheeks. He crumpled the handkerchief in his fist and slammed it against the headline. Breathing came no easier. *Home wrecking again? What more is there? Why are they doing this to me?*

He forced himself to read the article slowly, going over every sentence two or three times to understand what he was reading.

"*EXCLUSIVE: Dr. Richard Beecroft, Chairman and Chief Executive Officer of Whitecliff Laboratories, is at it again. Yesterday it was announced that Whitecliff had stepped in at the last moment to break up the Anglo-American marriage of International Pharmaceutical Products and America's Dolan Laboratories, apparently offering IPP's shareholders a sweeter deal. While Beecroft, who broke up his own marriage for the bodacious Page Three Girl, Fiona Hart (Centre Pages) . . .*"

Oh, God, no! Beecroft hurriedly turned to the center section, and there it was: a color photograph of Fiona in the left-hand columns, reprinted from fifteen years before. It was this photograph that, when unearthed eight years earlier by a Whitecliff employee, made Fiona Hart all the gossip of the Whitecliff staff. Further digging at Whitecliff turned up the fact that, for the first twenty-one years of her life, Fiona Hart wasn't Fiona Hart at all. She was born Mary McAfee, but had changed her name when she moved to London to help her launch her short, but now infamous, modeling career.

Inevitably, a senior colleague of Richard's exposed him to his new secretary's past, but, rather than causing Richard to replace her, the picture had the opposite effect—it captivated him, and he kept it locked in a personal file in his desk and referred to it often until, one evening, alone in the Whitecliff boardroom preparing for the following day's board meeting, Richard admitted to Fiona that he constantly felt the pressures of his job and couldn't imagine carrying on without her. When, without speaking, she reached for his hand, he worked up his courage to tell her that he'd seen the picture, had "marveled at it; had been aroused by it." Still without speaking, Fiona stood, locked the boardroom door and turned toward him. She was smiling and had already begun to undo the buttons to her blouse. He beckoned for her and she straddled his lap, pulled her blouse down her arms and let it drop to the carpeting. She kissed him and then reached to unlatch her bra, and then offered herself to him and grabbed him roughly by the hair on both sides of his head and pulled him to her. She kissed him again and whispered, "Are you sure you're ready for this, Dr. Beecroft?" and he thought he had never tasted such a full, warm mouth, a mouth that would hungrily follow her slow unbuttoning of his shirt and trousers, surprising and satisfying him beyond his wildest fantasies the many times he'd studied *The Galaxy*—alone, late at night, in the privacy of his office.

But now this picture of Fiona Hart—*Now my wife, for God's sake! Now Fiona Beecroft. Mrs. Richard Beecroft. Someday Lady Beecroft*—kneeling, her skin-tight blue jeans unbuttoned exposing her navel and her belly, her neatly arranged blonde hair and large blue eyes looking mannequin-like, her mouth open, the tip of her tongue wetting her upper lip, her hands cupping her full breasts with their rigid nipples—now this picture haunted him in a very different way.

His face began to warm and his heart began to speed again with ever-increasing force. His chest felt as though it were folding in on itself, tighter and tighter and tighter. He could not draw a full breath, nor could he keep his feet or hands still.

He looked from side to side out the windows of the car, then at the picture in front of him, then out the windows again. He drew several deep, audible breaths. He could not think what he should do.

"Are you all right, Dr. Beecroft?" his driver asked.

"Take me home." He folded his hands to control their shaking; unfolded them, then folded them again. "No," he said. "Let me out here."

"On the motorway, sir?"

"No, not on the motorway, you idiot." He opened his handkerchief with his trembling hands and wiped his forehead. "Yes, here. I can't breathe. I'm trapped," he whispered.

"Sir?"

"Please, take me home." He felt pressure building in his bowels. "Please, Mike. I'm not feeling well."

Richard lurched up the steps to his house, fumbled with his keys before unlocking the glossy maroon door and walked quickly to the bathroom, stripping off his raincoat and jacket and casting them on the floor, then undoing his belt and fly as he walked. He shut the door with a loud bang and heard Fiona call, "Hello? Hello? Is someone there?"

"It's me," he coughed out. "I'm in the loo."

He heard her call to him from outside the bathroom door. "Richard, are you all right?"

"I'll be out in a moment. I can't talk right now."

When he was through, he looked quickly in the mirror, smoothed his wet hair with his hand, and opened the door and stepped into the hallway.

"You look awful," Fiona said. "Was it something you ate?"

"No, it was *not* something I ate." He controlled his shaking hands by stuffing them in his pants pockets. He looked at Fiona, then looked away. He was still having trouble concentrating. He took a deep breath and looked at her again. Her neatly styled hair and large blue eyes matched those in the picture in *The Galaxy,* and repulsed him.

"Do you think you're coming down with something?" she asked. "The flu bug's going around, you know."

"You can be certain it's not the flu."

Fiona turned him toward her. "Then what is it? Richard, what's going on?"

Again he felt his chest tighten and found it hard to breathe. He stared blankly at Fiona and thought that she had humiliated him, that she may have spoiled his image forever.

"I've got a problem."

Fiona grabbed him by his forearms. "Has something gone wrong at the company? I knew it. There's a problem with that man Haney, isn't there?"

His heart began to race again. He forced out, "Nothing that simple. It's worse."

Fiona whispered, "Oh, my God, you've been sacked."

"No, I have *not* been sacked," he bellowed. "*We've* got a problem."

"*We've* got a problem?" Fiona's eyes turned an inky blue as they narrowed. "There was something in the press, wasn't there?"

"Yes."

"I'm involved?"

He nodded.

Fiona let go of his arms. "You promised me you would keep us—keep me—out of this." She stepped back and stared at him. His thinning hair and the chalky skin beneath it glistened with sweat. Sweat dripped off his nose to the floor. Sweat trickled down his temples, along his neck, drenching his collar. Large dark circles showed on his blue shirt beneath his arms. To Fiona he looked like he was ninety years old the way he hunched over every time he tried to draw a breath. "You're disgusting," she said.

He fumbled for his handkerchief and wiped at his face. "I didn't . . . I didn't *promise* you anything."

"Don't play word games with me, Richard Beecroft. You said you wouldn't give in to the pressure if it might involve us."

He tried to draw a full breath. "It was a calculated risk. You know," he choked, "a businessman's judgment call."

"And? And, Richard, and what?"

He drew short, audible breaths and looked away. "There was a picture."

"Oh, for God's sake! *What* picture?" she screamed.

"You know. *The* picture. *The Galaxy* dug it up."

"Oh, my God!" Fiona stepped forward, pressed her hands against her husband's chest and pushed him backward. "You promised me you wouldn't do this to me." She clasped her hands to the side of her head and pulled at her hair. "You've ruined me forever! How will you remedy this?"

"What can I do?" he said, and paused to catch a breath. He realized that he must gain control. Wasn't that what was expected of him as CEO? Moreover, how could he let himself be pushed around by a woman who, only a few months before, had been his secretary? "Be reasonable." He felt himself begin to calm. "What's done is done. And let me remind you that I didn't pose for that picture."

"You bastard!" she screamed. "My life was in shambles and I used the assets I had to do my own kind of deal, so I'm no different than you. I knew there were risks, but I needed the money. I wanted to stand out from the crowd if only for a moment. We've been all through this a hundred times, Richard. And let me remind *you* that you had no objection to that picture—quite the opposite, actually—when you began fucking me."

"Nonetheless, it was *your* indiscretion, not mine," he said. "And you certainly got your wish to stand out."

"Well, my second indiscretion was marrying a man who cares more about his reputation and doing deals than he does about his wife!" She pushed him toward the door. "Get out of here! Get back to your office where you know your way about. I can't stand the sight of you!"

Richard moved toward her and she stepped back. "You can't undo what's been done," he said. "It's just something you'll have to learn to live with."

"Learn to live with it? What about you? Or doesn't this concern *you*? Don't you care about me and the fact that I'm being humiliated by all of this? Or is it just your tramp of a wife who will have to learn to live with it? Is that it? How have things suddenly gone so terribly wrong? I married you for all the wrong reasons and now I'm the laughingstock of London. Well maybe I can learn to live without you!"

"Fiona, please. You're being unreasonable. It's ruined me as well." He reached for her.

"No. No, Richard," she said with a loud laugh, backing away from him. "No. Not until you've taken a bold step to make amends, and . . . and maybe not even then."

"But I told you. I don't know what more to do. The die is cast."

"You could begin by saying you're sorry."

"I've already told you I was sorry," he said, and thought that in time she would realize that things were as he described them; that what was done was done, and there was nothing more to be said. All he wanted to do at that moment was to get things back on track with Benson and the Prime Minister's office, and in a hurry.

"No. You didn't say you're sorry! You don't know how to say you're sorry. To say you're sorry means you have to care about someone other than yourself. And that's not you, Richard. Not you. So get back to your deals and your calculated risks, for this time you've got it right, you selfish, egotistical bastard: there is nothing more that can be done. You've put me in the gutter forever, and I can see no way out. I'm trapped. And you knew all along it would happen. You and Peter Benson and all the rest of you power-hungry bastards. All for the sake of a bloody deal."

CHAPTER 10

"That Fiona Beecroft is quite a piece of work, isn't she?" Nigel Finch-Hatton said with a knowing smile. "I assume by now you've seen *The Galaxy*."

Bud snapped open his briefcase and began flipping through the mound of papers in it. "Saw the picture; read the article."

"What do you Americans call a woman who looks like that? Arm candy?"

"Whatever it is, Richard doesn't deserve the press digging up twenty-year-old pictures of his wife without any clothes on."

"The picture is fifteen years old," Nigel said, "and she's wearing jeans. All that aside, Richard's traded up quite a bit from his first wife. Naomi was very capable, but she certainly wasn't much to look at; the exact opposite of Fiona and your friend JJ."

"What . . .?" Bud caught himself. He forced a smile, slipped his half-glasses in his shirt pocket, and rubbed his eyes with the knuckles of his index fingers. He patted his cheeks as though he were trying to wake himself, waiting—hoping—for his anger to subside. He pushed his chair away from the table and stood.

He and Richard had chosen The Stafford Hotel as a neutral site for their first merger-planning meeting because its small entrance court, tucked away from the busy streets of London and shielded by Green Park, made it unlikely that he and Nigel and Richard and his CFO would be seen entering or leaving the hotel. Earlier that morning, Nigel and he had been delivered in identical, late model black Mercedes sedans a half hour before the Whitecliff team was scheduled to arrive, and were now in a small, private dining room just off the hotel's main lobby, where he was doing everything in his power to control his rage. He breathed heavily and walked to the sideboard and lifted a cup, wondering if he would be able to pour coffee anywhere near it, his hands were trembling so. He took another deep breath and tried to steady himself. Over his shoulder he said to Nigel in as casual a fashion as he could muster, "Do you think JJ's incompetent or just unnecessary?"

Nigel rearranged the papers on the table in front of him. "Oh, she's quite competent. She's just too involved in our business and has too much influence with you for my taste. And, I've said it before: she and the others at GilbertBeard do little that my department can't."

"Except provide an outsider's point of view."

"I think she's a little too close to you to be considered an outsider."

"I'm not quite sure what you mean by that, Nigel, but let's leave it there." He spread his hands, watched them tremble, took a deep breath and carefully poured himself a coffee and walked back to his seat. He glowered at Nigel and waited for him to look up. "Is JJ all that's bugging you, or is there something else?"

"Well, yes, there is something else," Nigel said. "When we complete this deal, I think it would be an excellent time for me to . . . well . . . to step down, and let Whitecliff's CFO take over my job. He's got a good reputation and is well liked in The City. Also, he's quite a bit younger than I am. As a consequence, I was wondering how you might feel . . . what we might arrange."

"If what you're asking is: will I honor your contract, the answer is 'yes,'" Bud paused. "Nigel, if you help me pull off this deal, I can assure you you'll ride off into the sunset one hell of a rich cowboy."

Nigel let out a small sigh, a sigh that at first Bud interpreted to be one of relief, but quickly realized signified something else.

"Can I get that in writing?" Nigel asked.

"What in hell are you talking about?" Once again, Bud thought he'd like to throttle the son of a bitch. "Get *what* in writing? I just got through telling you I'd honor your contract. Jesus Christ, Nigel, what's going on with you? First you take shots at my investment banker and then question my integrity. I don't make hollow promises and you goddamn well know it."

"I'm not questioning your integrity," Nigel said. "I'd simply be more comfortable with something in writing . . . in case there's a problem." He leaned toward Bud with an arrogant smile that irritated him further. "You must now know as well as anyone that business situations can, and frequently do, change."

"What's happened? A man's word is no longer worth anything? There was a time when you did a deal with a handshake, remember?" He thought about the only thing he had in common with this man was the weather and was about to tell him he could take whatever it was he wanted him to put in writing and stick it up his ass, when he realized he'd just gone back on his word—his handshake—with David Dolan. He sat for a moment without speaking. "Okay, Nigel, you're right. Things can change. These days, no one's word is worth a tinker's damn. I'll sign whatever it is you need me to sign. But, from now on, keep your thoughts about JJ to yourself, you hear?"

Promptly at eight o'clock, Richard Beecroft strode briskly into the room, followed by two men. Before either Bud or Nigel could register their surprise, Richard introduced his Chief Financial Officer, James Lord, and his Chief Operating Officer, Bob Murphy. While Richard's colleagues settled in and arranged their documents, he moved to the sideboard, placed a croissant and a banana on a small plate, and poured a cup of tea. Bud stood and walked to him. "Richard, I thought we were limiting our teams to two a side," he said in a low voice.

Without looking at him, Richard said, "What ever gave you that idea?" He added two spoonfuls of sugar. "If you remember the Lazard report, this is a sixty-forty deal." He said this loud enough for the others to hear him and, staring at his cup as he slowly stirred his tea, he continued in a manner Bud thought sounded very much like a rehearsed response. "Seeing that you're here—that your Board has approved these discussions—I assumed that you had accepted the sixty-forty proposition. Given that, I thought it was appropriate for the majority partner to have the majority representation." He turned and looked first at Bud, then at his subordinates and smiled. "Representation that closely mirrors the deal structure."

"That's not the impression you gave me when we set this meeting up," Bud said quietly, still trying to keep the discussion between the two of them.

"If I remember correctly, I told you I was bringing my Chief Financial Officer," Richard said. "I never said I wasn't bringing anyone else."

Bud tried to calm himself. He didn't want Richard, or his negotiating team, to think that Richard had the upper hand but he wanted to send a signal that he couldn't be bullied; that he didn't deal in half-truths. "But you damn well *implied* it, Richard," he said. "And you implied we were coming together to discuss the management structure and the processes we were to follow. 'Collegial negotiations' is what you called this session. You don't have any surprises on *that* score, too, do you?"

"I can assure you, I am a man of my word."

"Aren't we all?" Bud said.

"And we *are* here for collegial negotiations. But I assume you understand one thing: the sixty-forty structure and equivalent management representation are *not* negotiable." Before he could respond, Richard asked, "Where do you stand with Dolan Laboratories?"

Bud walked around the table and sat. "I broke off the deal with them Wednesday night," he said, and added that it had been a pretty rough meeting. He regretted admitting it as soon as the words left his mouth.

"Pity, but, as you Americans say, that's why you're paid the big bucks. Now, shall we begin the collegial negotiations?" Richard said, still standing, sipping his tea, his close-set dark eyes avoiding Bud's angry glare.

The preliminary discussions concluded shortly after lunch. Since their contentious start, Bud and Richard had quickly agreed that eliminating duplicate functions was one of the major drivers in making their merger successful, and the next steps in the process were put in place, most of which would lead to *the* public relations nightmare for both men: job cuts, perhaps 15,000 of them.

"Well, other than one hell of a lot of hard work going forward, all that's left is putting the senior management team in place," Bud said. He looked at Richard and suggested that they get some fresh air and "take a little stroll around Green Park." Richard agreed and they hurried out of the hotel and through the covered walkway that led to the park. Richard clasped his hands behind his back, leaned into the wind and began taking long, rapid strides. "Whoa," Bud said. "Hold up a minute, will you, Richard. We've got some real important issues to wrestle with."

Richard stopped and looked down at him. "Such as?"

"You know as well as I do." He raised a finger each time he listed an item he wanted to discuss. "Your role as Chairman. Mine as CEO. Do we need a Chief Operating Officer? Who's going to do the finance job? Who's going to head up R & D? The make-up of the Board."

"From your less than spontaneous list it appears as though you may have some thoughts on the matter," Richard said, and began to walk slowly along the macadam path that circled the park, buttoning the top button of his black raincoat and pulling its belt tighter. He slid his hands in its pockets. "Well? Go on."

"Look, Richard, before we start, I'd like to get a couple of things straight between us. First, if we're going to work together—I mean really work *together*—I'd appreciate the hell out of it if there were no more surprises. It doesn't give me a lot of confidence that our relationship's going to be a productive one and, frankly, it really pisses me off." He waited for Richard to reply. "Well? What do you say?"

Richard looked at the path and kept on walking. "Noted."

"I guess that's better than nothing." He smiled and shook his head. "And on a real personal note, I'm sorry you and your wife had to go through all that stuff in *The Galaxy*. It must be awful rough on her; on the both of you."

Richard stopped walking, looked at Bud, then looked away. He pulled his tightly balled fists from his coat pockets, slid them back, and drew them out again. He looked at Bud once more, and then shifted his eyes to something in the distance. He drew a deep breath. "That's my business, not yours." He exhaled audibly and stammered, "What are you proposing for the top of the house?"

"Well," Bud said, "it's very important to me, as Chief Executive, that we get the organization right from the start." He searched Richard's face for a reaction to referring to himself as the chief executive but none was evident. Richard seemed to be somewhere else. "Richard, I'm asking one last time for confirmation. The day we sign the deal I become CEO and you part-time chairman."

Finally, as though he had just woken, Richard said, "There's no need to discuss that any further. It will be viewed as appropriate and received favorably by the media."

"I assume that's confirmation," Bud said. "Okay, let's start with finance. Nigel would like to retire and thinks James Lord would do a good job as CFO. Do you agree?"

He looked about the park, expressionless. "Yes. James will be well received in The City. Next?"

"Next is your man Bob Murphy. I don't want someone between me and the operations and would like to do away with Murphy's job."

"Agreed. It will be viewed as an attempt to streamline." A cold rain began to fall. "We'd better return to the hotel," Richard said. "We can talk about the other management appointments next week."

"Okay for now, I guess," Bud said as they turned, the rain blowing against their backs. "But I think we should discuss the makeup of the Board sooner than later."

Richard nodded. "Let me know by the weekend whom you recommend from your Board, and I'll do the same for mine. Is there anything else you would like to discuss, or is our 'little stroll in the park' completed?"

"You certainly do have a way with words," Bud said.

"And so do you, I might add," Richard responded, and they hurried toward The Stafford in a cold, wind-driven downpour.

As they entered the shelter of the covered walkway that led to St. James's Place and the hotel, Bud stepped behind Richard and followed him. He had expected resistance and met none, even on the difficult issues of Richard becoming part-time Chairman and doing away with the COO's position and the COO himself. *It's all how it's received—how it's perceived—that's the issue.* An uneasy feeling washed over him. *Did I paint Dr. Mickey Mouse into a corner? Or is he desperate not to do anything more that the press can pick on? Why do I get the feeling that we're far from through here?*—and he felt as if he was piloting a small plane over the ocean, flying farther and farther from shore, slowly getting too far from land to return home safely, and he thought about JJ's first law of wing walking, and told himself that in a deal of this size, of this visibility, after today's discussions with Richard, he'd better have a Plan B—and maybe even a Plan C—to grab hold of.

Not wanting to disrupt the fragile balance of their relationship and their decisions, he glanced up at Richard as they climbed the short set of steps to the hotel and said, "Onward." But, as he entered The Stafford and brushed the water from his raincoat, he was not at all convinced that he knew where "onward" would lead, or that he would be happy with his urging's final destination.

CHAPTER 11

Oblivious to the raw, blustery November weather, David and his father stood shoulder to shoulder on the lawn in front of the Princeton University Chapel, their dark suits buttoned once to keep their somber neckties in place against their white shirts, both graciously acknowledging the refrains of sympathy and kindness about Elizabeth from family and friends, and from the President of the university, chairmen of several pharmaceutical competitors and hundreds of employees and retirees from Dolan Laboratories. But the sense of calm that had come over David from this comforting outpouring of affection for his mother, and the concern showed for his father and him, was suddenly interrupted. He turned to his father and asked, "What's he doing here?" but Arch was talking quietly with his sister Sarah, her hands held tight in his large grip, and didn't seem to hear him. David looked to Susan who stood nearby and nodded in the direction of Bud Haney. "What does he think he's doing here?"

Susan put her hand gently on his arm. "I called him."

"You did what?"

"I knew he'd want to know about your mother, so we called him."

"We?"

"Samantha and I."

"Damn, Susan, I wish you'd—"

She squeezed his arm. "I thought you'd understand. It meant so much to the girls and you had so many other things on your mind."

"After what he did to all of us?"

"I called him for our family, not for the company." She smiled but her look begged for David's understanding. "And I don't think he's changed. He was devastated by the news and was so sweet with Samantha. So gentle. Give him a chance. Please?"

David looked across the leaf-strewn lawn where Bud and his daughters stood in a knot, Bud with one arm around Samantha's shoulders, his free hand alternately stroking the tops of Christi and Charlotte's heads. David could tell from the heaving of Samantha's back that she was sobbing. A fresh wave of sadness came over him when a familiar voice asked, "You okay, son?"

David blinked and focused on the man now standing in front of him. "I'm okay, Uncle Ben, it's just . . ." Once more he glanced at Bud and his daughters. Bud looked his way, caught his eye and smiled. David returned to his uncle. "It's just some unfinished business. I wish I'd had one last chance to tell Mom how much I loved her." His uncle assured him that his mother knew, that she thought he was all anyone could ask for in a son, but these warm words were quickly erased when he noticed Bud standing next in line, waiting patiently to greet him.

When Ben moved away, Bud stepped toward David and put out his hand. "I can't tell you how sorry I am for your loss.

Your mother was the loveliest woman I've ever known." David shook his hand; felt the familiar power of his grip, and then let it go. He stared at him without saying a word. He was aware that his hip and thigh had begun to burn. He wanted to speak, but didn't know what to say. He wasn't really sure what he was feeling. The man standing in front of him didn't look like a traitor; didn't look all that different from his great friend of the past, a friend who cared about his family. He struggled to make sense of all the conflicting issues, the ever-changing roles.

Bud stuffed his hands in the pockets of his raincoat and looked directly into David's stare as though he were trying to intercept his thoughts. "You've got to know how sorry I am about everything. Please, tell me you do and let me off the hook." David still didn't know how to answer. Bud stayed in place and, after a moment, said quietly, "It's okay, I understand," and moved away.

David turned toward him but, before he could speak, his father said, "Why, Bud, thank you for coming," and reached to embrace him, and David wanted to ask his father, then and there, how he could be so forgiving with this Judas but not his own son.

"I wouldn't have missed paying my respects for anything," Bud said. "I loved Mrs. Dolan a lot."

"And she you," Arch said. "Will you come back to Fox Hill after this is over?"

Bud glanced at David. "I . . . I'm afraid I can't, sir. I've got to get back to London. Things are a bit crazy at the office right now." He hesitated. "I just wanted you to know how sorry I am about Mrs. Dolan. Y'all have had more than your share of bad news lately and I'm sorry about the role I played in all of that."

"No need to apologize," Arch said. "All is forgiven. It's water over the dam."

Bud shook Arch's hand and nodded at David. "Y'all take care," he said, "You're in my prayers," and walked slowly toward Nassau Street where a chauffeur stood by a dark limousine waiting for him.

David watched Samantha run across the lawn, her long apricot-blonde hair streaming behind her, and heard her yell, "Uncle Bud, wait! You can't leave without saying good-bye." But before he, too, could call to Bud to wait, another mourner stepped in front of him and he wondered what he would have said if he *had* caught Bud's attention; and what he would tell his father once they were alone.

All is forgiven? Water over the dam? He wasn't so sure.

CHAPTER 12

Bud was in no hurry to meet with his Sunday evening dinner date as he strolled through the fashionable squares and along the gated parks that are the signatures of the exclusive Belgravia section of London. The cool November air, with its persistent hint of dampness, felt good to him, and his spirits were buoyed by the fact that he was making his way somewhere on his own, unaided by chauffeurs, pilots and flight attendants, unattended by members of his staff and all his many fawning consultants and advisors. He was content with this brief time to relax, to take a break from limousines, airplanes, hotels and meeting rooms and could feel his worries drop away and slowed his pace even further. He felt freer than he had in months but try as he would not to think about business, he continued to review all that had happened in the past ten days.

The stock markets on both sides of the Atlantic were surging ahead and the pharmaceutical industry was benefiting from what *The Wall Street Journal* called the "double whammy effect": a bull market combined with speculation of further mergers within an already attractive market sector. The Mercks, Glaxos, Pfizers and the big Swiss companies were reevaluating their competitive positions in response to the giant pharmaceutical juggernaut soon to be known as Whitecliff-IPP—frequently called "Dream Co" by industry analysts. *I'm in high cotton,* he thought. *Better than I have any right to expect. My options are worth £75 million and I'm going to be the lead dog in one hell of a big company. And everybody involved is getting richer by the day—hell, richer by the rumor—thanks to old Dr. Mickey Mouse and me.* As he walked past the Royal Mews for Buckingham Palace, he tried, once again, to probe why he'd never learned how to balance business and pleasure, and thought maybe it was because he'd never really been pulled to do so, although on this night thoughts of JJ tugged at him more forcefully than he would like, and he wondered how she viewed all that he'd accomplished—how she saw him on a personal level; and, once more, wondered if it had all been worth losing a friend like David Dolan.

He arrived at Number Sixteen Buckingham Gate at ten past eight. A butler showed him to the main room where Richard was waiting for him. Richard didn't offer to shake his hand but looked at his watch instead. "I was wondering for a moment if you'd forgotten our meeting." Bud found himself beginning to apologize for running late, but Richard interrupted. "Never mind," he said, and dismissed the butler with a wave of his hand and pointed to a small bar by the door. "Fix yourself a drink and let's get down to business."

Bud thought he noticed a slight tremor in Richard's voice. Something told him it would be best to approach this conversation with caution. He poured himself a beer, and raised his glass. "Cheers." He forced a smile.

Richard lifted his glass slightly and motioned toward two overstuffed chairs that flanked an ornate coffee table. The two men seated themselves opposite one another, and Bud began picking at a bowl of cashews on the table between them. "Well, Richard, what's on your agenda? I assume we're here to finish our conversation about the make-up of the Board."

Richard smoothed his tie with an open hand, pressing it flush against his long, thin torso. "That, and more."

"Fire away."

Richard smoothed his necktie again. "Putting the Board makeup aside for a moment, something's come up that I need to discuss with you."

"If there's a problem, I'm sure we can fix it," Bud said. "No matter what it is."

"I'm glad to hear you say that." Richard unbuttoned and rebuttoned his double-breasted blazer and centered his tie. "It comes down to this: my Board and I don't feel the proposed management structure reflects the sixty-forty nature of our deal."

"What the hell are you talking about?" Bud said. "I thought we'd agreed to all that on November nineteenth." Suddenly, he was reminded how quickly, and easily, Richard had agreed with him that rainy afternoon in Green Park, and it occurred to him that the whole discussion might have been nothing more than a pro forma performance. He felt his anger rising and asked Richard if he could be a little bit more specific.

"Of course." Richard looked directly at him for the first time. "Put rather bluntly, we've concluded that IPP has too much representation at the executive level."

Bud picked a cashew from the bowl and turned it between his thumb and forefinger. "But, Richard, we've already signed off on the management structure."

Richard straightened his long frame in his chair. "Tentatively."

Bud shook his head in disbelief. "No, Richard, not tentatively. It's what you and I agreed upon the day we met at The Stafford."

"Perhaps, but upon further reflection, once the deal is finalized, I'd like you to step out of the way."

Bud felt his heart rate quicken and pinched the cashew hard in his trembling hand. "I'm sorry, but I don't think I heard you right."

Richard did not divert his eyes. "I'm sure you heard me properly. You're to stand down as CEO."

Bud dropped the cashew back in the bowl. "Have you lost your fucking mind?"

"Quite the opposite. My management group"—Richard hesitated—"and my Board"—he hesitated again—"and I, all agree it's essential."

"What the hell do you mean 'essential'?"

"Essential if we're to have a deal."

Bud stood and looked down at Richard, and then seized him by the lapels of his blazer and jerked him from his chair. He stared hard into Richard's bewildered, shifting eyes, and jammed his lapels close against his throat. "You slippery son of a bitch! You haven't changed one fucking iota." He shoved him backward, sending him stumbling and spinning, finally grabbing for the chair back to regain his balance.

Richard straightened and ran a hand back over his hair. "Control yourself. For God's sake, man, control yourself!" He cleared his throat. "And please, move away."

Bud noticed that sweat had begun to trickle down Richard's temples and neck. "I'll stay put, thank you."

"Please, give me some room," Richard said, and took a step back. "What we're proposing is that Bob Murphy becomes CEO. At the end of the day, having Bob the Chief Executive better reflects our controlling interest in the business."

"And if I say no?"

"It's not negotiable," Richard said. "If you say no, there's no deal, although I need not I remind you that we have other options to bring your company under control. But, don't worry, no matter what, you'll be very well taken care of. Very, very well indeed." Richard took a deep breath. He appeared to relax slightly. Bud thought he even smiled. "Besides, you've had a good run. Better than a man of your caliber should expect."

Almost without a sound, other than the guttural growl that accompanied the blow, Bud's left fist caught Richard's right eye squarely in its socket, causing Richard to spin away, stumble a few steps and drop to his knees like a large rag doll, his hands covering his face.

Bud stood above him, waiting for him to say something. Slowly, Richard opened his hands in front of him as though he were expecting a gift and studied the blood that covered them. His eyelid was already discolored and swollen almost completely shut. Blood seeped from the slit of an opening onto his cheek. "Help!" he called. "Please, help."

Bud walked slowly to the door, wondering what Richard could say—what he could say—that would end this nightmare. As he reached for the doorknob, the butler pushed open the kitchen door. When he saw Richard kneeling on the floor—staring at his crimson hands, his right eye purple and grotesquely swollen, one side of his face streaked with blood—his mouth dropped open. "My God, Dr. Beecroft, what has happened?"

"He'll be all right," Bud said. "He's just a bit clumsy, that's all." He turned in the doorway and watched the butler grab a napkin from the dining table and hand it to Richard. "Is there anything else you want to say, Richard? Want to change your mind?" When Richard didn't answer, he said, "Because I'm not changing mine." He looked at the butler and then back to Richard. "Y'all have a good night."

It was raining when Bud stepped from Whitecliff's corporate hideaway. *A soft evening, isn't that what they call it? Well, a soft evening my ass. It's been rough as a cob.* He pulled up the collar of his blazer and walked quickly to the shelter of the doorway to The Bag O'Nails pub. He hurried inside, ordered a pint of Guinness and sat in an empty booth. He held his hands palms down in front of him, studied the swollen red knuckles of his trembling left hand, and took a deep breath to calm himself. He clasped his glass with both hands and stared across the crowded pub. *What in hell got into me? "You've had a good run. Better than a man of your caliber should expect." That's what got into me. Well, I'm dead in the water. I've fucked up the deal and fucked myself in the bargain. How will I ever justify breaking off two deals to the financial community? And what the hell do I tell my Board? You and your goddamn temper. Goddamn ego's getting as big as all the rest. But hand my people over to that lying son of a bitch? No way. The Board will understand. They can't agree to get in bed with a snake like Beecroft. And what do I tell JJ? Well, honey, I lost my goddamn temper and punched the SOB in the most critical moment of my career because I'm a hotheaded redneck?*

He stood, leaving his Guinness untouched, and walked toward home. Near Eaton Terrace he began to jog, thinking he couldn't let this merger slip through his fingers, couldn't afford to cut off two deals in two weeks. The rain became heavier, soaking his hair and running into his eyes. He ran through Sloane Square and down Sloane Street to the Brompton Road, where he slowed to a walk, then ran again, then slowed once more, as he wrestled with what he planned to do.

He stopped as he approached Alexander Terrace, hoping he could remember Richard's address from the Royal Opera

House fund-raiser he had attended there the previous fall. He walked slowly and studied the small row of houses. *The maroon door. That's it! The one with the maroon door.* He crossed to the far side of the street and looked at the house. The first floor was dark, but several rooms on the next two floors were brightly lit. He saw the silhouette of a woman pass in front of one of the second story windows. He waited a moment to see if Richard was home as well. *Next thing you know, you'll get arrested for being a peeping Tom. Wouldn't that be a fitting ending to this lousy fucking night?*

He walked across the street and up the small set of steps to the maroon door. He raised his hand to ring the buzzer, took a deep breath and pushed the small ivory button. A woman's voice crackled through the speaker box. "Hello?"

"Mrs. Beecroft?" he said.

"Yes?"

"Is Dr. Beecroft home? I'd like a word with him."

"Who is this?"

"It's Bud Haney, Mrs. Beecroft. I'm a colleague of Richard's, and I'd like a quick word with him, if it's okay."

"Just a minute. I'll be right down."

He lowered his collar and ran his fingers through his wet hair, trying to make himself look more presentable. He heard the dead bolts inside unlock and the door opened. "Please, come in," Fiona said, and then laughed. "You look like a drowned rat."

She moved aside in the narrow hallway to let him pass, then shut the windowless door behind him. She wore open-toed white angora slippers, blue jeans with a narrow gold belt cinched around her waist, and a snug white v-neck tee shirt. Her image in *The Galaxy* flashed across his mind. He drew his hand from his pocket and offered it to her. "Ma'am, I'm Bud Haney—"

Fiona took his hand and smiled up at him. "You're not at

all the way I imagined you. You're so much nicer looking than the way Richard described you."

"I'll bet," he said.

"Oh, don't worry about what Richard says. I know all about you men in business. And it's not 'ma'am.' We save that for the Queen. I'm Fiona."

"It's nice to meet you. I was wondering if Richard—"

She interrupted him. "What kind of an accent is that?"

"I'm a southerner."

"But the people in Disney World didn't talk like you."

"No, ma'am. I'm from Alabama. Florida's a different kettle of fish. Is Richard—"

"Well I find it soothing." She cupped her hands together. "Now, what can I offer you? A cup of tea? A drink? And, please, take off that wet jacket before you catch your death of cold."

I've just punched her husband silly and she's offering me a drink? "No thanks," he said. "I'll only be a minute. Has Richard gotten home yet?"

"No, but he called from the hospital and said he'd be home shortly."

Bud took a step backward toward the door. "Well, I won't keep you, but would you please tell Richard I stopped by to apologize and see if we couldn't keep on talking."

"Apologize?"

"He didn't tell you?"

"Tell me what? He was so full of his fall and banging his eye on the steps at Buckingham Gate that he never mentioned you."

"Oh," Bud said. "I've . . . I've made a mistake. It was just some business stuff. I'm sorry to bother you."

Fiona grabbed his sleeve. "What are you talking about?"

He looked at the floor. "Nothing, ma'am. I'd better get—"

She held firm to his wrist and asked, "What happened tonight?" She placed her other hand on his arm and lowered her eyes. She drew small circles on his sleeve with the nail of her index finger. "Please. I want the truth."

Bud swallowed. "The truth is . . . the truth is we had a disagreement and I lost my temper, and I'm real sorry I did."

"You mean he didn't trip on the stairs?" She tightened her grip on his sleeve and the blue of her eyes brightened. "It sounds exciting. Tell me, please."

"You really want to know?"

She answered quietly that she did.

"Well, okay," Bud said. "Your husband said something that really got my goat and . . . and I punched him."

"It sounds so violent. I never would have guessed that about you."

He nodded. "Well, now you know, and I owe Richard an apology, and you one, too. So, if you would, please tell him I stopped by."

He turned to leave but Fiona held fast to his arm. "You're a rare one, Bud Haney: a warrior who cares about who he hurts. I'd like to know more about that; about you. Richard doesn't care about anybody."

Bud tried to slip by her, but she took his wet lapels in her hands and moved closer to him. "I don't plan to tell Richard you stopped by. He'll be happier living with his little lie, and I'll have a secret of my own." She smiled up at him. "And you could have one, too."

He took her hands and pried them gently from his lapels. "There's no need for you to get involved in this mess, Mrs. Beecroft. I'll call Richard tomorrow. This is our problem, not yours."

Fiona pulled her hands free from his and pressed them against her cheeks. Her large blue eyes grew cold and narrow. "Don't be so sure. His dealings have a way of affecting me too."

Bud nodded. "I understand."

"I'm sure you do." She smiled at him again. "When this is all over, maybe we can talk further."

"Maybe." He wished her goodnight and let himself out. By the time he'd reached the sidewalk a silver Jaguar sedan had pulled to the curb across the street and Richard's driver had opened the rear door and Richard was slowly working himself free from the car. A white gauze bandage, held secure by a large X of adhesive tape, covered his right eye. He closed the car door behind him. "What do you want now?"

"I stopped by to see if you were all right and to ask if—"

"Of course I'm all right." Richard looked past him. Fiona stood in the open doorway, her features in shadow from the hall light that shone behind her. "What did you tell her?"

"I told her you'd taken a spill and I wanted to check on how you were doing."

"Well stay away from me, and mind your own business." He brushed by Bud and pointed a finger at him. "I never want to hear from you or see you again."

Bud turned to face him and, as he did, he heard Fiona's voice calling quietly. "Richard. Oh, Richard. He told me what happened. He came to apologize."

"You'd listen to this hooligan?"

"At least he told me the truth and handled it like a man. That's more than I can say for you," she said. "It was a matter of image, wasn't it?"

"You don't know what you're talking about," Richard said.

"I'm afraid I do, Richard, dear. And I now know that your image is all that matters with you."

"Well, bully for you, the one who's done a fine job of destroying it."

Bud watched Richard climb the stairs to his house and slip past Fiona, and then watched the light shining on the stairs close to nothing as she shut the door. He turned to Richard's driver who stood against his car with his hands folded across his crotch as though he was guarding himself against a football penalty kick. "I don't suppose you'd be headed in the direction off Eaton Terrace," he said.

The driver shook his head. "I don't think Dr. Beecroft would approve, sir."

"You've got a point," Bud said. He couldn't help but laugh. "Well, have a good night."

"And you, sir."

Once home, Bud stripped from his wet clothes and pulled on a terry cloth bathrobe. First he called Nigel and then Chris Pearson leaving both a message to meet him the following morning at Chester Square at seven sharp, "come hell or high water."

He lay on his bed and dialed JJ. He was disappointed when her answering machine picked up and left her the same message that he'd left for Nigel and Chris, but added that things had gone badly in a meeting with Richard. "So please, JJ, once again, drop everything and meet me for breakfast. I . . . I need your help. I think I've screwed up . . . screwed up but good."

He had never spoken to JJ like that before. He had always simply listened to her advice and given her assignments. It was never anything but business with him—plans, strategies, finance—strictly business. But now he had asked her for help and had admitted he was human. Worse yet, he'd left a message that he couldn't erase—a message that violated his code of conduct. He chalked this small sign of weakness off to fatigue and stress. *It'll go unnoticed by her anyway,* he hoped, and switched off the light.

CHAPTER 13

Nigel and JJ were greeted with a nod from Bud, his hands stuffed in his jacket pockets as he paced at one end of the dining table while he waited for the butler to finish serving the first coffees. When Alberto was through, Bud told him he needed a few moments to talk with Miss Jennings and Mr. Finch-Hatton before breakfast. Alberto gave him a knowing nod and JJ a subtle bow, and excused himself.

Bud waited for the kitchen door to click shut and then looked at Nigel and then at JJ. He found an unexpected level of comfort as he looked into JJ's questioning brown eyes. "To cut through all the damn suspense," he said, "Richard's up to his old tricks. Last night he threw a wrench in the works and basically killed our deal."

JJ dropped the spoon she was using to stir her coffee. It ricocheted off her saucer with a sharp clank onto the tablecloth. "Sorry," she said, "but you've got to be kidding. Not two busted deals in as many weeks. This can't be happening"

"It's happened."

Nigel raised his eyebrows and, Bud thought, looked very—*very*—disappointed, perhaps even a bit panicked. "I assume there must be some . . . some misunderstanding . . . and some recourse. Perhaps Richard's trying to negotiate a better deal."

"There's no misunderstanding," Bud said. "Certainly not on my part, and not on his, either. And I don't believe this was a negotiating ploy. Old Richard simply changed the terms of the deal at the last moment. He screwed us, but good."

"Oh?" Nigel said. "How so?"

"Simple. Ugly, but simple. He told me I was to give up becoming CEO or we didn't have a deal."

"Oh, no," JJ said. "And after all that you two—"

"And what did you say?" Nigel interrupted.

Bud's account of his meeting with Richard was detailed and complete. He frequently quoted Richard verbatim, although he thought it best not to admit to having lost his temper. He rubbed his hands together, checking his left to make sure there were no telltale signs from the night before. "There was nothing I could do but say no," he concluded. "It was a total breach of faith. And, what's more, he refused to offer any options other than a veiled threat to take us over."

"Damn, Buddy," JJ said, and patted him on the arm. She glanced at Nigel with an embarrassed look and quickly folded her hands in her lap. "I know it will come as no surprise to either of you, but when this news gets out, a lot of people are going to lose a lot of money."

"I should say," Nigel mumbled.

"And there's going to be hell to pay in The City and on Wall Street," JJ said. She stared at Bud. "You're soon to become public enemy number one because Richard is sure to lay the blame at your feet."

"But goddamn it, JJ, Beecroft reneged on the deal. He's the

one who didn't act in good faith. He screwed *me,*" Bud said "That's got to count for something."

"Listen to me for a moment." JJ pushed her coffee cup forward, replaced her spoon neatly in its saucer and clasped her hands on the table in front of her. She spoke slowly and softly. "No one will care if Richard screwed you, or if you screwed him. This isn't about who's right or wrong, or good or bad. All anybody will care about is that the deal's dead and IPP's and Whitecliff's stock will have both tanked as a result. The fund managers and your other shareholders will say somebody screwed *them,* and that *somebody* will be you, the high-paid American fat cat with his £2.5 million pay package and his umpteen millions of pounds of stock options; you, Bud Haney, whose ego will be viewed as too big to step aside in the interest of your shareholders. The funds will be calling for your head in a heart beat to get you out of the way so the deal can go through."

"Who in hell's side are you on anyway?" Bud asked.

JJ looked surprised and hurt. "That's not fair," she said. "You know as well as I do. I'm *your* banker. Remember? I'm just trying to do my job and advise you objectively." She paused. "You know I'm right, don't you?"

He nodded.

"Of course Richard won't go unscathed either," she continued. "You know how much the press likes to scorch him and bring up his wife's past. But the fund managers will see you as the roadblock between them and the deal, no matter how wretchedly Richard Beecroft handled you. And so will the press." She turned to Finch-Hatton. "Right, Nigel?"

Her question seemed to interrupt Nigel's silent deliberations. He sputtered, "Yes, of course. Yes . . . yes. A lot of people are going to lose a lot of money on this turn of events. Not to mention all of us."

Bud felt himself flush but struggled to keep calm. He was angry and disappointed with Nigel, but not surprised. "This is no time to be thinking about saving our own skins."

"Although that's exactly what you did last night," Nigel said.

"That was different—"

"Isn't it always when it comes to our own situations?" Nigel said.

"Nigel, listen to me, will you, goddamn it!" He pounded his fist on the table. "Beecroft changed the rules. That's the difference—"

Before he could finish, JJ jumped back in. "Frankly, I'm as worried about how your Board's going to react as I am about the financial community."

Bud abandoned his attack on Nigel because JJ had raised the topic that was of the most concern to him. "I've given that a lot of thought, and I don't see any other way to handle it than to tell them exactly what happened. I think they'll view it as a matter of principle. I doubt they'll agree to continue doing business with someone as untrustworthy as Richard. And I think they'll be persuaded that, without me as CEO, the deal's an outright take-over by Whitecliff. Do y'all agree?"

Nigel shook his head, seemingly lost in thought.

"I hope for your sake you're right," JJ said. "But I don't think it's necessarily going to go that way. They might take the position that no single person is bigger than this deal. Besides, I'm sure they're going to be worried sick about being sued by their shareholders."

"I don't think they'll be that weak if I bring them into it early, explain it to each of them personally." It was at this point, as he listened to his plan in his own words, that Bud realized he'd have to work hard to convince his Board to see things his way, that he was in a life-or-death struggle to save face, to save his job, to save all that he'd devoted his life to for the past twenty-five years. He turned to Nigel who still seemed to be daydreaming. "Nigel, you with us?"

Nigel nodded.

"Okay, if you could rally a trusted group at IPP House and start thinking about a Plan B—first off drafting what we might say in a press release about why the deal collapsed—it would be a big help. If you'd do that, I'll wait here to give Chris the news and ask him what he'd like to do about the Board. If all goes well, I should be in my office about ten and we can see where we are then."

Nigel stared blankly at his boss, stood and walked to the door. "This is *very* bad news for all of us. Let's hope something can be done to get this deal back in place."

Bud ignored his comment. "I'm sorry I got angry with you, Nigel, but I'm between a rock and a hard place and I'm counting on you to help me." Nigel turned to leave and Bud wondered if the only thing that would save the deal would be for him to quit. *That's what old Nigel wants,* he thought. *That and all the money he'll make if I turn tail and the deal goes through.* He smiled at JJ and let out a deep breath. "Some pickle, huh?"

"Some pickle," she said. She fumbled with the top of the coffee pitcher and refilled their cups, poured herself some cream, and then moved her spoon in a slow, deliberate circle, staring at her coffee. "Buddy, I'm worried. Very worried."

"About what? And please don't call me 'Buddy' when others are around. It sends the wrong signal."

He waited for her to look at him, but she continued to stare at her cup and muttered, "Sorry." Finally, she looked up. "I'm worried about your Board and the financial community, but I'm more worried about the tone of your message last night. You sounded like you were in trouble. What exactly did you do that makes you think you screwed up so badly with Richard?"

"Hell, I don't know, JJ. I told him he'd lost his mind and stuff like that. Called him a bunch of names. Pushed him around a bit."

"Pushed him around a bit? What are you talking about?"

"Whatever I did, there's no way now he'll ever do this deal as long as I'm involved."

"You didn't hurt him, did you?"

He didn't answer.

"Did you?"

Bud looked down at his coffee and nodded.

JJ pressed her hands hard on her straight brown hair and ran them back over her head. "Bud Haney. You and your hot-headed . . . I don't know what."

"JJ, you've got to understand. I was devastated. Confused. Pissed as hell. Hey, I'm fifty-four years old, got a late start in this business, and don't have much time left. I've worked all my life for an opportunity like this and that snake Richard went back on his word. And what's more, JJ, he insulted me; said I'd had a good run, better than a man of my caliber could expect, and I hit him. Just once, but pretty good."

"Oh, my God," JJ whispered.

"Look, I'm not proud of it. I'm not a thug, and I don't want you to think I am. I don't go around punching people, but he was messing with me personally—messing with every-thing I've ever worked for—and I snapped. And I think he planned to dump me all along. I was nothing more than a pawn to get his deal this far."

JJ shook her head.

"You don't agree with what he said, do you?" he asked. "About the caliber of man I am?"

She continued to shake her head. "Just know this: from this point forward, *everybody's* going to have their knives out for you. Beecroft. Nigel. Maybe even Chris Pearson. And some members—maybe *all* the members—of your Board. Not to mention the press and everybody in The City and on Wall Street. Right now, you don't have a friend in the world, and you'd better start thinking and behaving that way. Do you hear me? You don't have a single ally."

"Not even you?"

JJ collected her briefcase and got up from her chair. She stood over him; close enough for him to reach for her, to wrap his arms around her narrow waist, to pull her to him. To hold her. To tell her that *she* had to be on his side; that she couldn't agree with Richard Beecroft. To tell her how much he needed her; that she was the only friend he needed through all of this; that with her he'd be just fine. Instead, he pushed back from the table, straightened his legs and crossed them at the ankles, and jammed his hands in his pants pockets.

JJ looked down at him. "I've got to get to my office. I've got a lot of thinking to do. A lot of worrying to do."

He fixed his eyes on hers. "I'll ask you again, JJ. Where are you and I on all of this? I have a right to know."

She took a step away from him, then a second. "I've been your investment banker for two years and, as always, I'll do anything I can to help you and your company. That hasn't changed. That's my job."

He pushed himself from his chair and stood.

JJ started for the door, then turned. He thought she might be crying. "No more. No more questions. Not now. I've got to go."

Before he could tell her that he didn't like her answer worth a damn, that he wanted to know where he stood with her, once and for all, she had left.

Like rats off a sinking ship. He smashed his right fist into his open left hand, sat and rested his elbows on the table. *I can't lose her, too.* Slowly he reached for the small silver bell in the middle of the table and rang for Alberto. He thought he might as well have breakfast while he waited for his Chairman, *the next potential traitor,* to arrive.

"What can I get for you this morning, Mr. Haney?" the butler asked.

A friend I can trust, he thought, and smiled. "I don't think you have what I need out in the kitchen, Alberto, so why don't we just settle for a bowl of porridge and some brown toast."

CHAPTER 14

Chris Pearson fished a small box of matches from the pocket of his suit jacket, lit a thick Romeo Y Julieta cigar, and blew a cloud of bluish-gray smoke toward the crystal chandelier above him, signaling that the time had come. The four men seated at the table adjusted their chairs and waited for him to expand on his guarded comments about the breakdown in negotiations with Whitecliff Laboratories. Chris, in turn, watched impatiently as the waiter poured coffee. "That will be all for this evening and please make certain that we aren't interrupted."

"Port, sir?" the waiter said.

"No," Chris snapped. "That will be all." He looked at his watch and signaled the man to the door with two short waves of his hand.

On this cold, wet London night, the five men huddled around the dinner table at White's Club were all non-executive Directors of IPP: their host and Chairman, Sir Christopher Pearson; Euan MacDonald, Chris' right-hand man, once

Chairman and Chief Executive of Blue Oval Industries, and now Vice-Chairman of IPP; Sir Peter Jensen, the retired Chief Executive of Thames Transport; Dr. Paul Jones, the distinguished Welsh cancer research specialist who had recently won The Queen's Award for Innovation; and Göran Lundberg, a highly-successful Swedish entrepreneur appointed to the Board to represent the European Union point of view. IPP's two American directors, Richard Novak, Chairman of Allied Diagnostics, and Roger Ross, founder of Ross Information Systems, were absent, although Novak was flying to London from New York as his colleagues met at White's. Ross had offered his apologies for his absence, citing "an unfixable personal conflict" as his excuse.

Chris rotated his cigar slowly between his fingers and studied its lengthening gray ash. "Now, gentlemen, down to cases. As I told you earlier, Richard Beecroft has asked Bud to step out of the way once our deal is finalized. Moreover, he told him that if he didn't cooperate, the deal was off, although he implied that he had other options. One of those options could be a hostile bid for our company, and I wouldn't put it past him. Given the press he's been getting lately, I think he'll do anything to pull off this deal."

Chris paused and looked from man to man. "In turn, Bud told Beecroft, in no uncertain terms I might add, that he wouldn't step down." He paused for a moment, drew on his cigar and blew smoke toward the ceiling. "To be thorough and fair to all, Richard then personally insulted Bud and, in the heat of the moment, I'm afraid Bud hit him—and a pretty good blow, at that."

A number of the Directors shook their heads in disapproval. Euan MacDonald smiled. "Good for Bud. If we can't trust Beecroft to keep his word on something as important as who the CEO is, how can we trust him with our company?"

Chris cocked his head toward MacDonald and placed his cigar carefully in an ashtray. "Euan, I don't think it's quite that simple. While I admit it may have been satisfying for Bud's ego, it wasn't the best thing for our company or our shareholders. I've already told him it was unprofessional at best, and put us all in a compromising position, at worst. So that's the situation. My objective tonight is to educate you on all sides of this issue in preparation for our deliberations tomorrow."

The Directors began asking questions in rapid succession.

Is the deal really dead?

Can it be brought back on track?

Why had Beecroft taken this stand?

What happens to our stock price if we don't do the deal, and what about shareholders' suits?

After all this, can Beecroft and Haney work out their differences?

"As far as the deal being dead is concerned, I believe that decision lies with us," Chris answered. "Other than that, I can only answer parts of your questions. To begin with, there's been bad blood between Bud and Richard in the past, and apparently it's surfaced again. However, Beecroft's stated rationale never touched on their inability to get along. What he told Bud was that Whitecliff didn't have adequate management representation. Or, put another way, IPP had too much control with Bud as CEO."

He tapped the ash from his cigar. "And so, gentlemen, because these are unusual circumstances, with your permission, I'd like to make an unusual request: I'd like us to be briefed by Nigel and our advisor from GilbertBeard about the financial community's probable reaction to different scenarios."

Chris paused to let what he was suggesting sink in. "I've asked Nigel and JJ Jennings to join us so that any bias I might have won't influence your thinking. Obviously, their participation will require the utmost confidentiality. Do I have your approval?"

All bowed their heads momentarily to reflect upon Pearson's request. When they looked up, one by one each nodded affirmatively and their demeanors changed almost instantly, going from somewhat titillated by the Haney-Beecroft clash and its dramatic outcome to dead earnest. Chris thought it was a though he'd thrown a switch causing his Directors to suddenly realize that *they* were accountable for IPP's future; that it was time for *them* to step up and truly earn their directors' fees. As he sensed this change of attitude, he no longer worried that his unusual scheme of holding this secret briefing might alienate them. Just the opposite. Upon seeing their reaction—how it had focused their minds—he was convinced that he had done the right thing, that they were no longer merely corporate hood ornaments.

He pushed his chair from the table, strode across the room and opened the door. Nigel was waiting outside, hands clasped in front of his dark suit, a hint of a smile on his face. JJ stood behind him, holding a thick gray binder with the distinctive rose-colored *GilbertBeard* script centered on its cover. Chris beckoned for them to come in.

The Directors nodded at Nigel and more than one smiled at JJ who searched for a place to stand to address the group. Chris slid his chair from the head of the table to make room for her. "I think most of you know our principal contact at GilbertBeard, Miss JJ Jennings." He, too, smiled at JJ and then gestured to Nigel to begin.

Nigel greeted the Board formally and said he had agreed that GilbertBeard should present them with an objective view of what the reaction would be if IPP "reneged" on the Whitecliff deal. He cocked his head at JJ, sat and folded his arms across his chest.

Several Directors shared confused looks at the curtness of Nigel's remarks as JJ placed her unopened binder on the table. She paused for a moment, ran her hands down her hips and the outside of her thighs to smooth her dark blue skirt, and thanked Chris for the opportunity to speak to his Board. "Before I begin, I'd like to comment on what Nigel just said." She looked at Finch-Hatton and gave him a curt smile. "If you decide not to proceed with Whitecliff, and if you position yourselves properly, *Richard Beecroft* will be viewed as the one who reneged on the deal, not Bud Haney." She paused. "Nonetheless, in the end the financial community won't be looking to place specific blame. What they want—above all else—is the deal."

Nigel started to say something, but Pearson's shake of the head stopped him.

JJ continued. "Having said that, the math and the probable outcome of not doing this deal with Whitecliff are pretty straightforward and predictable. What you decide to do as the Board of Directors is a far more complex task.

"The math exercise begins on the first of November, before IPP publicly entered into discussions with Dolan Laboratories. At that time, your shares had been trading fairly consistently around six hundred and fifty pence here in the UK, or fifty dollars a share on the New York Exchange. Those are key reference points for you to remember. Six hundred and fifty p, and fifty dollars."

She made eye contact with each Director and then gave a detailed account of IPP's share price performance at every critical point since November 1, and concluded, "So, at the close of business today, since you began talking about merging, first with Dolan, then with Whitecliff, IPP's shares have increased thirty-eight percent."

She looked at Nigel who seemed to be staring into some

far off space, although all others present appeared riveted by what she was telling them. She smoothed the lapels of her dark jacket, and continued. "So, gentlemen, the sixty-four thousand-dollar question is: what will happen to IPP's share price if you don't go through with the Whitecliff deal?"

Two Directors moved their chairs closer to the table and leaned toward her. The room was silent except for the occasional groan of a diesel engine as a taxi passed in the street below.

"I think the answer comes in two parts." She tapped the tips of her index fingers together. "First, if you stop negotiating with Whitecliff, and second, if you can't restart discussions with Dolan."

The Directors nodded in agreement, and encouragement for JJ to answer her sixty-four thousand-dollar question, which to them was more like a sixty-four *billion*-dollar question, the approximate market capitalization of IPP.

"So, here's what I think. If you stop the deal with Whitecliff, your share price will drop fifteen to twenty percent, and, I might add, there may well be shareholder suits as a result. Further, if you can't restart discussions with Dolan, your share price will drop another eight to ten percent. All in all, without either of these deals, almost immediately your share price could be a third lower than it is today."

"A third? Do you really mean a third?" Peter Jensen asked.

"Yes, and I think that's the figure you should base your discussions on, because I think it's highly unlikely—out of the question, really—that your company can re-establish an amicable relationship with Dolan Laboratories."

When asked why she adopted that position, JJ briefed them on phone calls from David Dolan to her management saying there was no way—"until hell freezes over"—that he would ever deal with Bud Haney or IPP again.

"So, there you have it," she said. "Without these deals we

predict your shares will drop precipitously, from nine hundred pence to six-eighty in the UK and from seventy dollars to less than fifty-five in the US."

Chris thanked her and asked if there were any questions.

Euan MacDonald said, "Yes, Chairman, there sure as hell are." He looked at JJ, his bushy gray eyebrows twitching nervously, his half-glasses dangling by a tartan neck-cord on his barrel-like chest and, in a thick Scottish brogue, asked, "What you're telling us is we have to decide whether we support Bud Haney, and watch our share price tumble, *or* support the deal with Whitecliff and sacrifice Haney. Isn't that the nut of it?"

For a moment, JJ didn't answer. She folded her hands behind her and shifted her weight from one shiny black pump to the other. Her silence drew even more attention than her summary of the financial realities. When she finally did address MacDonald's question, her answer was barely audible. "Yes, sir. That's your dilemma."

"And what would you do if you were us?" Nigel asked.

The Directors seemed surprised that Nigel had spoken. It was, after all, a meeting of the outside Directors and Finch-Hatton was present only to give financial advice, not to participate in the debate. "That's a question for your Board to answer, Nigel, not your investment banker," she answered.

"But you must have a position on all this," Nigel insisted. "Surely you've discussed it, and this meeting, with your friend Haney. I know very well how you look after him."

At first JJ gave Nigel a quizzical look, and then said that she had *not* discussed the meeting with Bud because Chris Pearson had asked her not to. "Besides, Nigel, Bud's nobody's fool. He doesn't need me to tell him what decisions your Board is faced with. He understands what's at stake here as well as, if not better than, anyone in this room."

Chris tapped his cigar on the ashtray. "This isn't particularly helpful, Nigel. Let's move on. Are there any more *financial* questions for JJ?"

The Directors indicated that they had no further questions.

"Very well, then," Chris said. "Thank you, Nigel, for joining us, and thank you, JJ, for a very targeted summary. It's been a most helpful session."

JJ collected her binder, said goodnight and opened the door, but Nigel remained seated. Chris gestured for him to leave. "You're excused as well," he said. "I'd like some more time with the non-execs."

"I understand," Nigel said, "but could I have another moment with the Board before leaving?"

JJ closed the door quietly behind her and muttered, "Whore," and then, "Yes, sir, that's your dilemma." She slapped her GilbertBeard binder against her hip. "Sold Buddy down the river for a lousy banker's fee, all in the name of sound fiscal advice. I'm nothing more than a two-bit whore." She walked quickly down the worn carpeted stairs and through the lobby and onto the street and into a heavy downpour. *Of all the nights to forget my umbrella.* She raised her hand to hail a taxi, the rain matting her straight brown hair and soaking her dark blue suit. She waved frantically at each passing cab, and then watched Nigel open the door to a chauffeur-driven Mercedes and nod at her as he stepped into the car. She shook her head in dismay as the car pulled slowly from the curb, leaving her standing in the drenching rain, her hand raised like a schoolgirl seeking permission to ask a question. She thought what a bastard Nigel was and that she'd just aided and abetted the enemy, and for what? *For nothing more than a lousy banker's fee.*

CHAPTER 15

While the IPP Board was secretly being briefed at White's Club, Bud Haney was preparing his comments for his meeting with them the next day. By ten o'clock he felt he was as ready as he'd ever be and dressed for bed and slipped beneath the covers. His briefcase sat open on the bed beside him. He drew his calendar from it to review his activities for the week. He ran his finger down the page for the following day—Thursday, December 2—and tried, yet again, to assess the magnitude of his secretary's simple inscription: *BOD meeting-IPP House,* when he noted that Joanne had written *Samantha's 17th birthday* at the top of the facing page.

"Ah, shit," he said aloud, "it's my goddaughter's birthday." He checked his bedside clock. *Just a little after five in Princeton. Maybe she's home from school by now.* He reached for the phone and dialed the Dolans' home number. It rang twice before a man answered. He hesitated. "David?"

"Yes."

"It's Bud."

David said he recognized the voice.

"Sorry to bother you," Bud said. "I thought you'd still be at the office. I was calling to wish Samantha a happy birthday."

"She's not home."

He waited for David to say more. When he didn't, he asked when a good time would be for him to call back.

"She'll be around this weekend."

Again, he waited for David to say something, and, again, there was nothing but silence at the other end of the line. Finally, he said, "Have you got a moment for me?"

"I guess."

"You'll never know how much I hated myself for calling off our deal."

"You've already said that. At the Four Seasons, remember?"

"I've replayed that conversation over in my mind a thousand times. I thought I was making the right business decision and thought—maybe just hoped—you'd understand. What I didn't take into account was what it would do to our friendship; and to your family."

"But you should have known."

"You're right. I should have known. And you should know, better than almost anyone, I've never been one to grovel, so cut me some slack, will you? I mean how many ways are there for a man to ask a friend for forgiveness?" He paused, once again hoping for David to answer. When he didn't, Bud said, "The irony of it is, I may have cut you off for nothing."

"What are you talking about?" David said.

"I can't give you the details, but old Dr. Mickey Mouse is messing with me but good. If you think I betrayed you, wait until you see what Richard's done to me. I'm afraid I've fucked it up all the way around."

"Jesus, Bud, I've never heard you sound like this."

"That's because I've rarely been like this. I'm in deep shit, David. You'll know just how deep in a day or so."

"I'm sorry to hear that."

Bud thought there was a sudden softening to his tone. "Sounds like we're beginning to bury the hatchet."

"It'll taking some getting used to," David said. "I'm trying to do the same with Dad, but it isn't easy. Far from it." He cleared his throat. "So, yeah, we're burying the hatchet. Just never forget what a terrible setback your decision was for me, for all of us."

"I won't forget it. Believe me, I won't."

"Okay," David said. "It's history. As Dad says, time heals all wounds."

"Let's hope he's right."

David laughed. "He'll think he is, no matter what."

"Hey, things will work out with you and him. You'll see. He wouldn't know what to do without you but has a real hard time acknowledging it. I think losing your brother kind of froze him in time and he takes his grieving and anger out on you. You're just a scapegoat, that's all."

"Maybe. It's a nice thought, anyway."

"Well, it's time for me to get some sleep before I meet my maker," Bud said. "Tell Samantha I called and I'll try her again over the weekend, and give my love to Susan and the young ones. And thanks for talking with me. It's meant the world to me."

"And me," David said. "We're back on track." He wished him luck, told him to stay in touch and said good-bye.

Bud exhaled a deep breath and took one last look at his calendar. He was drawn again to the notation: *BOD meeting-IPP House* and his sense of relief from his conversation with David seemed to slip away like water through his fingers. He tossed his calendar into his briefcase, snapped it closed and set it on the floor beside his bed. He turned out the light and lay on his back with his hands clasped behind his head and stared into the darkness, wondering where JJ was on all of this. He rolled on his side, wrapped his arms around his pillow and drifted into a fitful sleep.

Seated at the head of his boardroom table, he thought the meeting was going very well. He admired the table's highly polished, deep mahogany luster. *Smooth and thick as ice,* he thought, *and I'm very comfortable in this high-backed leather chair!* He liked the supple cordovan leather and massaged the chair's arms with the palms of his spread-fingered hands. Feeling secure in his high-backed chair, his seatbelt forming a snug X across his chest, he smiled at his Board and swiveled the chair from side to side. Left to right. Right to left. Left to right. "Richard Beecroft reneged on our deal. Reneged, Goddamn it, do y'all hear me? Reneged!" He looked around the hexagonal table—*Smooth and thick as ice. It seems to tilt with every swivel of my chair*—looked at his Board of Directors and wondered if they would support him. He smiled. "That smug bastard asked me to step down or there's no deal." He smiled again and comforted himself further in the soft leather of his high-backed chair. *Things are going great!* He nodded at the people seated around the shiny mahogany table: Chris Pearson, Nigel Finch-Hatton, and the others—and for a moment he thought he recognized David Dolan, and smiled at him. A red light began to flash above the meeting room door, and the highly polished table nosed downward and canted to the right. Bud struggled with his controls. He saw the explosions before he heard them. *Flak and SAMs!* Meeting papers began to curl at their edges, lift off the table and swirl above the heads of IPP's Directors, then rush past him. *An 8 1/2-by-11 blizzard!* He laughed. Coffee cups spun by him. He wanted to catch them but held steadfastly to his controls. "Gentlemen," he said, addressing those seated at the table as their Chief Executive Officer, "we're taking on enemy fire." Chris Pearson shook his head as though he couldn't hear above the antiaircraft flak exploding now in small black clouds close by. "Step aside, Bud. Step down," someone yelled above the roar. *Perhaps they don't understand. The bastard screwed me!* He thought if he spoke louder, with a little more authority, they'd understand. "How can we trust a man who goes back on his word?" he yelled over the explosions. The men tucked their ties inside their jackets and held them against their shirts to keep them from blowing with the wind. Thick black smoke began to stream from beneath the far end of the table, surrounding Chris Pearson, who buttoned and re-buttoned his double-breasted jacket while Bud struggled with the controls, the joystick forcing his hands toward his crotch then toward the instrument panel in violent spasms. "Mayday! Mayday! I'm hit!" he said, and then calmly notified his Board of Directors of his coordinates. "It looks like our next meeting will be held somewhere in the Tonkin Gulf." *Can they hear me?* "In the fucking Tonkin Gulf!" he screamed above the hammering of the explosions. Smoke filled the boardroom. He reached above him and pulled the ejection seat handle. *Get your ass out of this mess! Find Plan B!* Instantly, he was free from the table, blood inching in slowly spreading, frothy-pink streaks across the visor of his helmet. He swayed beneath his parachute—*Quiet, so quiet! Not a sound—just the groaning of the risers.* He watched his crippled A-4 Skyhawk, its swept-back starboard wing shot completely away, right itself. *Without me, for Christ's sake! It's flying without me, without Lieutenant Junior Grade Bud Haney!* Beneath him, on the bank of a narrow, muddy river, he could see the five-foot-square bamboo cage. *Home again! Comforting, like my high-backed leather chair.* He drifted slowly over the cage, swinging right to left, left to right, the relentless, cold rain now drenching the back of his flight suit. He squinted through his blood-streaked visor and for the first time—*or is it? He's always there!*—He saw the thin, buck-toothed

Vietnamese boy, dressed in a black shirt and black pants and Day-Glo green shower shoes, grinning and pointing an AK-47 at him, its curved gun-metal gray clip and large front sight flashing in the sun. He tried to wave the boy away, his hands knotted against his sides by his bed sheet. He swung to the left and when he looked back, JJ Jennings stood in the boy's place at the edge of the river, beckoning toward him with her delicate hands, then cocking the AK-47 with a sharp, business-like *chunk-chunk* and leveling it at him. David Dolan swam in a circle in the dirty water in front of JJ, looking up at him and screaming, over and over again, "Welcome home! Welcome home!"

Bud struggled to get himself free, his left hand slamming against the clock radio, knocking it clear of the bedside table and onto the floor. "No!" he screamed as he wrestled with the sheet to sit upright. "Not this time, you bastards. Not this time!" He was shivering, his pajama top soaked with sweat. He took a deep breath, and then another, and switched on the light and ran his hands back over his wet hair. "I'm okay. I have not been recaptured. I am in my bed in London. I am okay," he recited to himself mechanically. He leaned forward and picked the clock from the floor and replaced it on the bedside table.

He walked to the bathroom, switched on the light and pulled off his wet pajama top. As he dried the sweat from his head and torso, he turned and looked at his back in the mirror. The nine long scars—souvenirs of his stay at the Hanoi Hilton—showed a dead white. He sighed. *Out of the frying pan, into the fire.* He flicked off the light and, as he walked back to his bed, had the ominous feeling that his dream was more a forecast of the future than a reminder of the past. *I really may be caught in friendly fire,* he thought. He lay on his back and stared into the darkness, reviewing the events and his actions that had mired him in his dilemma, and lay awake until it was time to get up and face his Board of Directors.

CHAPTER 16

The hastily convened Board of Directors meeting was scheduled to start at ten o'clock. An arsenal of equipment had been placed at each Director's assigned station around the highly polished, hexagonal table: a leather-bordered blotter complete with heavy paper for note-taking; two freshly sharpened maroon lead pencils with the IPP logo embossed in gold on one facet; bottles of sparkling and still water; and a heavy crystal tumbler. In addition, three black, pyramid-shaped microphones were spaced about the table, and two oval speakers were placed strategically, one between Chris Pearson and Bud Haney's seats, the other at the opposite end of the table.

The non-executive Directors arrived one at a time and set their briefcases and newspapers on a narrow credenza and, as though they were about to begin some form of manual labor, all removed their rain-spotted black and navy raincoats and their jackets and folded them carefully across the empty chairs that lined the boardroom walls. When they had poured their coffee or tea they seated themselves in thickly padded cordovan swivel chairs. None brought any papers to their seats for this was a meeting of judgment.

Pearson, Haney, Finch-Hatton and the company Secretary entered as a group. Nigel and the Secretary were in their shirt-sleeves. Chris kept his chalk-striped double-breasted jacket fully buttoned. Bud also wore his suit jacket, wanting to look as formal and as gravely serious as possible.

Once seated, the men passed a maroon leather-bound ledger from one to another, the cufflinks of their freshly laundered white and blue shirts occasionally clicking against the table's polished surface. The book was opened to a page that read, *Meeting of Directors held at IPP Headquarters, Hammersmith, on 2 December.* Beneath the line that read *Present,* Bud quickly scrawled his signature and handed the ledger to Nigel. "This should be one hell of a meeting," he said, breaking the silence. Nigel smiled briefly—sheepishly, Bud thought—signed his name and passed the ledger on.

Chris glanced at the large digital clock above the coffee service. He nodded and tapped the table with the butt of his pen to get his Board's attention. "Gentlemen, let's get down to business." Instantly the room went silent. Chris leaned forward and pulled a microphone closer to him. "If this is working, we should have Roger Ross on the phone in South Carolina. Roger, are you there?"

"I'm here," Ross said through the speaker. "Just keep pouring coffee for me, Chris. It won't be light here for another two hours."

"Very well. All present or accounted for," Chris said. "We only have one agenda item this morning, gentlemen, and that's the disposition of our deal with Whitecliff." He turned to Bud. "It's your meeting."

Bud pushed himself from his chair, buttoned his jacket, and walked to the front of the room. He put his hand on two

Directors' shoulders as he passed behind them and looked from one Board member to another. He had talked to all, either in person or over the phone, and they had, to a man, seemed supportive of what he was about to recommend.

In the fifteen minutes that followed, he reviewed the events that led up to his breaking off negotiations with Dolan Laboratories and beginning discussions with Whitecliff. He was factual, accurate, and brief. Frequently, several Directors nodded as he covered a particular point. As always, Peter Jensen, one of the longest serving members of the Board, was having difficulty staying awake. *Nothing new here,* he thought. *So far, so good.*

Next he described his fateful Sunday evening meeting with Beecroft and, for the first time, began to editorialize, calling Richard a "snake in the grass." He spoke openly of his frustration and admitted to hitting him. "I tried to apologize to him, but he wouldn't have any of it." He paused. "I owe all of you an apology, too, but I can't tell y'all how devastated I was by Richard's message. To begin with, *he* initiated the discussion about us merging and all along I had his assurances that he'd do anything—*anything at all* were his very words—to see that the deal did not fail. And, I had his agreement that I'd be able to represent our employees' interests as CEO.

"So my people worked their butts off day and night to make this dream come true and then, bingo!—Richard pulls the plug on me. And insults me to boot. But he didn't only pull the plug on me, but on all those folks who worked so hard to make this merger a reality." He looked at each Director as he said, "He also pulled the plug on all of you who supported this deal. So, I'm angry and disappointed. Who in their right mind wouldn't be? Frankly, I felt abused, and I felt my people had been abused, as well. It's clear to me now, and I kick myself for not picking up on it sooner, that Richard never intended to construct a merger of equals. What he wanted to do was take control of us. Having sixty percent of the equity wasn't enough; he had to have *his* man in the top job, too."

He looked around at the Board and felt he was in the midst of men who understood. Comforted, he moved on to the history of IPP's share price. "But, gentlemen," he concluded, "the issue here is not only our share price. The pivotal issue is one of trust, something you can't put on your balance sheet or pay a dividend with, but something you must have to build a great company."

He paused and searched each Director's eyes. "Richard Beecroft is not to be trusted. He hasn't dealt with me—or *your* company—in good faith. Further, I have no reason to believe that he will do so in the future. Consequently, I'm loath to turn the reins of this great company over to him. It wouldn't be fair to our fifty-three thousand employees, my management team, our customers or our investors, and for one simple reason: they could never trust a word the man says."

He drew a deep breath. "We're always wary of the irrational competitor, but in this case I think our concern about an irrational partner should be even greater. So, what I'm asking for, gentlemen, is permission to tell Whitecliff that we have ended negotiations with them, no matter how severe the financial repercussions are that follow. They're not the only oyster in the stew, and we can always pursue other options."

He slid his hands in the pockets of his suit coat and fixed his eyes on his Chairman. "May I have your permission to proceed?"

Roger Ross, the Director in South Carolina was the first man to speak. "You have my blessing, Bud."

One down, Bud thought. *Three more and I'm home free.*

Ross' voice came through the speakerphone again. "Chris, could you hear me? I said Bud has my vote to call off the deal."

None of the other Directors said a word. Finally, Chris leaned toward his microphone and said, "I heard you, Roger."

Bud bent his knees and shifted his weight forward. He wondered why no one else was speaking. Chris placed his fingertips together and touched them to his lips. "Thank you, Bud, for a very informative update. What I'd like to do now is have some time with the non-execs. So, if you and Nigel and our good Secretary would excuse us, we'll call you back as soon as we've had time to deliberate this very unusual turn of events."

Bud looked at Chris in disbelief. Nigel was already out of his chair and striding toward the door. The Secretary made a few hurried notes and excused himself. Bud remained at the end of the table, staring at his Chairman.

"Bud?" Chris said, nodding toward the door. "If you would, please."

"What the hell's going on?" he said. "What do y'all have to discuss that can't be said in front of your Chief Executive?"

Chris nodded toward the door a second time. "If you would be so kind. I need to talk to the non-execs openly, without any bias. I'm sure you understand. There's a lot at stake here."

Outside the boardroom two-dozen serious-looking people, all but one a man, all in dark suits, stood in small clusters, talking in hushed tones. JJ paced among them, her head down, occasionally bumping into lawyers from Slaughter & May, financial advisors from NatWest, or representatives from the IPP Investor Relations and Public Relations staffs. "Sorry," she muttered, as she continued to pace back and forth across the hallway. All stopped talking when the boardroom door opened and Nigel and the company Secretary, and, finally, Bud, appeared.

He shut the door and turned toward the questioning faces. "It looks like this meeting's going to last a bit longer than I thought, so everyone can get back to their offices." He asked Nigel and JJ to stay for a moment, then smiled and waved at the group. "I'll let y'all know when I need you. Just be patient, please."

When all were out of earshot, he said, "What in hell's going on? What's this closed-door session all about?"

JJ looked at the floor and dragged the toe of her black pump across the carpet. "I can only guess what's going on, and it's not good. This doesn't look like it's going to be the slam dunk you'd hoped it would."

Bud looked to Nigel, and the contained smile on his face annoyed him, but—for a moment at least—he ignored it and asked, "What's happened, Nigel?"

Nigel didn't answer.

"The deal falling apart is what's happened," JJ said. "And a lot of people want it put back on the rails."

Bud threw his open hands in front of him in frustration and mock surrender. "But Beecroft's the one who reneged on the deal, not me."

JJ grabbed him by his sleeves like a small child. "Listen, for once, and please, try to get this through your thick head: who's good and who's bad isn't the issue here. Your Board's concerned about two things: the share price and their own hides. Right now you're nothing more than a highly paid hired gun. A good one, but an expendable one. I know it's tough for someone like you to accept, but that's the way things are."

Bud gently removed JJ's hands from his arms and turned toward Nigel who was still smiling, causing him to finally boil over. "Nigel, two questions: One, do you agree with JJ? And, second, what in God's name is so funny?"

Finch-Hatton stopped smiling. "Of course, I agree. Your cowboy morality may be charming, but it's terribly naive. The only important thing here is our share price and how well the

Board protects it. That's *their* report card. I also agree that everyone is expendable, and that includes you . . . and me. But we'll have a bloody rich retirement as a result of all this, so why not relax and enjoy it?"

Bud dismissed Nigel's comments with a shake of his head. "Relax and enjoy it, my ass. Listen, I talked with every one of those men before this meeting and they all seemed to be with me, at least until today. So I ask you both again, what in hell has happened?"

"I sold you down the river," JJ said.

Instantly Nigel paled and took a few steps back.

"What are you talking about?" Bud said.

Nigel raised a hand to silence JJ but she ignored him. When she finished recounting the Board's dinner meeting at White's Club, Bud turned to Nigel. "You were there, too? Why didn't one of you tell me about this? Were y'all planning on keeping this a secret forever? You set me up." He looked from one to the other. "Goddamn it, JJ, you of all people! What's gotten into you?"

"I was doing what I'm paid to do," she said. "I don't like it any better than you do, but I was doing my job."

"Selling out on me is part of your job?" Bud said. "Well, you've done damn fine work of it."

"Rubbish," Nigel said. "Absolute rubbish. Chris wanted an objective evaluation of our situation and I used our most trusted advisor to deliver it." He looked at Bud as though he finally had the upper hand. "Chris also asked us to keep the meeting confidential, and he is, after all, our Chairman."

Bud glared at JJ. "Most trusted advisor? No longer. I thought you were . . . you were . . . hell, I don't know what I thought you were."

She asked if he couldn't understand the predicament she'd been placed in. She pleaded with him to try.

150

He shook his head in disgust and looked at Nigel, and then at JJ. "Y'all can go now," he said quietly. "You've more than answered my questions. If I survive this, I'll . . . I don't know what the hell I'll do . . . most probably fire you both. If I don't get out of this with my hide . . . then God have mercy on the poor bastard that's got to deal with you next."

"Well, gentlemen, all except Richard and Roger have had a night to sleep on this, and now you've all heard Bud's perspective and recommendation," Chris said. "So the proposition remains the same: pursue the deal with Whitecliff or support Bud Haney." He nodded at Richard Novak, who had made a curt wave of his hand.

"This may sound like a stupid question," Novak said, "but are you sure there can't be a deal that includes Bud?"

Chris said yes, he was certain, that he'd spoken with Beecroft earlier that morning. "Richard continually stressed that his management wouldn't stand for an IPP executive running what they believed would still be their company. Moreover, at least twice he said that he can't work with Bud but would be interested in talking further if, in his words, 'we removed that ruffian from the equation.' He did add, however, that he and his Board were also meeting this morning and would be looking at other options."

"That means the deal's off no matter what?" Novak pressed.

"Knowing Richard and the pressure he's under from his Board—and the Prime Minister—I can't imagine that would be the case," Chris said. "I think if we removed Bud, Richard would jump at the deal."

With that comment, the debate among the Directors began. At first it centered on what was in the best interest of their shareholders and the sticky question of shareholders' suits, and then moved to whether or not Britain would benefit from the deal. "One could argue that Britain would be better off with *no* deal," Euan MacDonald said, "because there won't be all the job losses."

Personal assessments were made. Concerns were expressed about sacrificing a CEO of Haney's caliber, about turning the company over to someone as distrustful as Richard Beecroft. Again, Euan MacDonald's forceful voice filled the room. "We must also consider our employees. We must do what's right for them as well. The proper course of action is to turn Beecroft aside and look for other opportunities. In the long run I'm sure our shareholders will benefit."

The Board's reputation was touched upon. If the deal didn't go through, how would they be viewed? As pawns for management? Reckless with their shareholders' interests? And again, the discussion circled back to shareholder value and how the Board would explain its decision to the institutional investors who would lose billions of pounds as a result. And the question of shareholder suits persisted.

"Positioning this correctly if we don't go through with the deal will be very dicey," Chris admitted. "Explaining why one man—a man who happens to be one of the highest paid in Britain—should take priority over what has been called the 'deal of the decade,' will be difficult. Not impossible, mind you, but difficult, nonetheless." He looked around the table. "Any further questions or comments?" All signified they were ready to move on. He leaned toward the microphone. "Roger?"

"I think you've covered it," Ross said.

"Well, gentlemen," Chris said, "then the time has come. So, if I may, I will simply ask you to vote whether you are for proceeding with the deal with Whitecliff, or against it." He glanced at the company Secretary. "Then we can make it a formal resolution, if need be." He paused a moment to give his Directors time to settle themselves. "Fair?"

The Directors agreed.

"Before we begin, may I remind you all that a member of this Board, Nigel Finch-Hatton, our CFO, would vote *for* the deal," Peter Jensen said.

"Aye, and we've got another member—our Chief Executive, for God's sake, Peter—who would vote *against* it," Mac-Donald said. "Let's keep this even-handed."

"Right," Chris said. "Let's keep it even-handed. What we do here will not only affect our share price but a man's career as well." He cleared his throat and leaned toward the microphone. "May I start with you, Roger?"

"Fine with me," Ross said. "I'm against the deal because I'm vehemently against doing business with a man like Beecroft."

"Thank you, but could we limit our comments to a simple 'for' or 'against?'"

"Okay," Ross said. "That's a simple 'against.'"

Chris forced a smile. "Peter?"

Jensen mumbled, "For."

"Paul?"

Jones voted for.

"Göran?"

"For. It's a matter of—"

"Please, Göran, let's stick to the rules," Pearson said. "Euan?"

"Damn well against. I don't care about shareholders' suits—" Chris raised his hand to silence him "—or anything else for that matter. We'll find a way to make this up to our shareholders, and I think the dust will settle fairly quickly."

Chris looked at MacDonald and gave a short nod, then turned toward Richard Novak. "How do you vote, Rich?"

"I think we owe this deal to our shareholders, so I vote we move ahead."

For a moment, Chris closed his eyes and massaged his temples. "Well, the Board has spoken, and the majority of Directors, four in all, have voted to proceed with the deal. So that's our decision. Thank—"

"One minute, Chairman. We haven't heard your vote," Jones said.

"It's not relevant," Chris said. "The majority has spoken."

Ross' voice crackled through the speaker, "But how would you have voted if we were tied? You owe us an answer as our chairman."

Chris put his hands on either side of his microphone as though he were trying to steady it. "I would have voted to support my CEO, and I'll—"

"Four to three!" MacDonald barked. "Doesn't anyone want to reconsider? This is a wrong-footed decision!"

"That's one man's opinion," Jensen said.

"Three men's," MacDonald said.

The boardroom went silent.

"Have I lost you?" Ross asked over the speaker.

Chris shook his head.

"We're still here," MacDonald said. "At least I think we are." He looked at Pearson. "Chris?"

Chris seemed startled to hear his name. "In deference to Euan's passion and long service on this Board, I will ask his question of all of you: does anyone want to change his mind, or does the vote stand?"

"I'm still against the deal," Ross said over the phone. The remaining Directors also said their votes hadn't changed.

"Very well then, we've reached our decision," Chris said, "and, of course, this is a unanimous decision." Jensen, Novak, Lundberg and Jones nodded affirmatively.

"Bloody hell," MacDonald said. "It's not."

"But we must portray it that way," his chairman said.

"If you must," MacDonald said, "but when you announce Bud's termination announce my resignation from the Board as well."

Chris began to say something, when Roger Ross interrupted him through the phone. "Add my name to Euan's."

MacDonald let his glasses drop on their lanyard and looked at Pearson. "And you, Chris?"

"I'll stay to see the deal through, and I don't think it's in the company's best interest for any of us to resign right now. At the rate the deal's been moving, those who want to should be able to step down in a few weeks' time. I'd strongly suggest that's a better way to proceed."

"I'll hold off until the deal's done," Ross said.

Chris looked at his Vice-Chairman. "Euan? For the good of the company?"

MacDonald nodded. "Aye, for you and for the good of the company."

Chris smiled for the first time that morning. "Thank you, gentlemen. Thank you very much. Any further business?" All signaled no. "All right, if you'll excuse us for a moment, Euan and I will talk with Bud and then we'll reconvene to plan how we move forward."

Bud was surprised when the door to the boardroom opened and a grim-faced Euan MacDonald appeared followed by an equally sober Chris Pearson who said Euan and he would like a word with him. The three men walked slowly past the long row of IPP's executive offices. Several secretaries, seated in front of the offices, began to greet them, saw the strain on their faces and looked down at their desks to avoid the men's eyes as they passed.

"Is everything okay?" Bud asked as they entered Chris' office.

MacDonald shook his head, walked to the window and stared out at the gray London morning. Chris shut his door and placed his hand on Bud's shoulder. "The Board has decided to pursue the deal."

"You chose Beecroft over me?"

"No," Chris said, pulling his hand from his shoulder. "We chose the deal over a guaranteed crash of our share price."

"Over me," Bud said again. "Everyone?"

"It was a unanimous decision," Chris said softly.

"Oh, for Christ's sake," MacDonald said, still facing out the window. He turned and looked first at Chris, then at Bud. "Let's put all the corporate posturing aside for a moment and talk like men. We didn't all vote for the deal. You had strong support from Roger and me, and from your Chairman." MacDonald stuffed his hands in his pants pockets and walked toward Bud, his heavy frame slumped forward. "I think we've made the wrong decision and so does Chris, but that's the way the vote went. I know it's hard for you to accept, but don't take it personally. Everyone feels you've been an outstanding CEO."

"Goddamn, Euan," Bud said. "Can you hear yourself? In an instant, I've lost my job, my reputation, my pride and a twenty-five-year career, all because some slippery prick changes the rules at the last moment, and you're asking me not to take it personally? Does that fucking compute?"

"No," Chris said, "it doesn't. But it's going to have to. I'm sorry, Bud. You deserve better."

"Well, I have some advice for y'all before the door hits me in the ass," John said. "The Board's decision is the Board's decision, but y'all had better tread real carefully with old Richard, because I don't think he's through with us yet. And while you're at it, I wouldn't take my eye off that two-faced son of a bitch Finch-Hatton for too long either."

Before either could respond, Bud put out his hand to Chris. "Thanks for your support. You're a good man." He shook his Chairman's hand and reached for Euan's. "You too, Euan. You're both damn good men. Now, if y'all don't mind, I'm going to take a little walk around the building and head on home."

He stopped at his secretary's desk on the way back to his office. Joanne looked up at him and smiled. "I hope the meeting went well. You've had several calls from Miss Jennings on her mobile. Shall I try to reach her?"

"Not right now," he said, and suddenly, angered and hurt beyond all comprehension, he felt like a trapped animal. He wondered just how far Nigel had taken his treachery, but most of all he was confused and infuriated by JJ's part in his demise. Instinctively he reached across the desk and took his secretary's hands and held them tightly.

"What's going on?" Joanne asked. "Is everything all right?"

Bud drew her to her feet and nodded toward his office. "We need to have a little chat, Jo. I've got some bad news for you. For both of us."

CHAPTER 17

For the first few minutes of the drive to Eaton Terrace, neither Bud nor his driver spoke. Bud studied the familiar landmarks along the motorway as though he might never see them again, and then stared at the carpeting on the car floor and wondered how he'd lost so much in so little time. His confused, angry thoughts again skipped from his Board's decision, to Nigel's selfish, untrustworthy behavior, and then to what he viewed as the greatest injury of all, JJ's outright betrayal.

"How did the meeting go, Mr. Haney?" his driver asked.

"Short. To the point. The merger's still on track."

"I understand, sir."

He caught Steve's eyes in the rearview mirror. Long ago he had learned that "I understand, sir" was Steve's way of telling him that he knew more—or knew better. "What do you understand?" Bud asked.

Steve glanced at him in the mirror. "That things didn't go well for you, sir."

"The word's already out?"

Steve kept his eyes on the road ahead. "It's gone through the building like wildfire. Mr. Finch-Hatton told his secretary and . . . well you know the rest. You know how it works."

"Good old Nigel," Bud said. "That no good son of a bitch."

"Yes, sir. The very same."

They rode in silence for the rest of the trip. Once parked on Eaton Terrace, Bud reached to the seat next to him and lifted his briefcase while Steve picked up his chauffeur's hat from the passenger's seat, and both men got out of the car. "Well, Steve, thank you for everything; for being such a good friend."

Steve shook his hand. "May I say something, sir? Something off the record?"

Bud said of course he could. Steve took off his hat and held it against his leg. "We all know you tried to do what's best for us and, no matter what comes of it, we'll soldier on as you would want us to."

Bud felt his throat crowd with emotion. "That's what I'll miss the most, Steve. That attitude and the people." He looked at his driver for a moment and then placed his hand on his shoulder. He could feel his eyes filling with tears and told himself to get control. "You take good care. I'll be in touch." He turned and climbed the steps to his door. As he sorted his keys he became aware that Steve was still standing where he had left him. He gave him a quizzical look.

"We really have seen a lot haven't we, Mr. Haney?" Steve said.

"Enough to fill a lifetime."

Steve put on his hat and saluted. "All the best to you, sir. *All* of us wish you the very best." He turned and walked back to his car.

So this is how I say goodbye to the whole shooting match, Bud thought. *To twenty-five years of hard labor. It's not the way I envisioned it. Not at all.*

Inside his house, he climbed the stairs to his bedroom and checked his phone. A large red **4** blinked up at him from his answering machine. He punched the message button. "It's me. They told me at your office that you've headed home. Please call as soon as you get this. I'm in my office now and I'll be home tonight. I've got so much I want to explain, so call as soon as you pick this up. Please?" He stopped the machine and erased the message. He had made up his mind that he wouldn't talk with JJ no matter what, and was in no mood to talk with anyone else. He lay on his bed, crossed an arm over his eyes and tried to plan what he would do next—not in future days, weeks or months, but that afternoon. He'd never been out of work before and, for the first time in his life since being a prisoner of war, time weighed heavily upon him.

He looked in the mirror and muttered, "The lead dog one minute; roadkill the next." He had just run a five-mile loop through Trafalgar Square, trying to sweat his problems away. When he finished drying his head and neck he threw the damp towel hard at the clothes hamper, pulled on a gray *Crimson Tide* sweatshirt and sat on the edge of his bed and mustered the courage to check the eight messages on his answering machine. He circled his hand tentatively above the machine, exhaled loudly, and pushed the PLAY button.

"Bud, it's David. I tried you at the office, but they said you'd gone for the day. Call me at work when you get this. It's important."

He wondered why David Dolan was calling, but his thoughts were interrupted by the lilt of a familiar Indian voice.

"Mr. Haney, it's Lakshmi. It's most urgent you call Sir Christopher. He must talk with you right away."

The next three messages were also from Chris' secretary. "What in hell's going on?" he wondered aloud.

The sixth message was from Chris Pearson himself. "Bud, I've been trying desperately to reach you. I've got some very disturbing news that I was reluctant to leave in a phone message, but now I know of no other way to get it to you before our press release goes out. You were right, Richard wasn't through with us. Far from it. When I called to tell him that our deal was back on track, he said that his Board had determined that a merger with us had some fatal flaws and that they were no longer interested in pursuing a deal with us. He said an outright acquisition, rather than a merger, would be better for them if they could find the right partner—"

He punched the STOP button. "That son of a bitch!" He stood and slapped his hands against the thighs of his warm-up pants. "That no-good son of a bitch! He screwed me and now he's screwed my company. What in God's name will he do next?" He clasped his hands on top of his head and turned in a circle. He felt the anger and confusion of earlier in the day return. *I was right. It* was *a matter of trust. I'm glad I hit the son of a bitch.* He placed his hands on the windowsill and leaned forward to stretch his hamstrings, grunting as he angrily overworked them. *Good old Dr. Mickey Mouse. Nothing ever changes, and yet . . . everything has changed.*

Across the street, lights in the stately white houses were beginning to come on like warm, bright pieces being added to a puzzle. He watched a neighbor park an olive drab Range Rover at the far curb, step from it, draw his briefcase from the back seat and climb the small set of steps to the shiny black door at number 32.

Home, he thought. *Home from work. Home with his family.*

Well, I'm out of work for the first time in my life, and I don't have a place I can call home. Or a family. Suddenly, he felt like a prisoner again—isolated, trapped, helpless, confused and with no one to talk to—and wondered what he might have done differently. "No sense crying over spilt milk," is what his doctors had told him. *Move on, Lieutenant Haney. Move on.*

He sat on the bed and took a deep breath. He was overwhelmed by Chris' message but was drawn to hear the rest and hit the PLAY button again. "I tried hard to change Richard's mind but he wouldn't budge; said this new strategy met all of his objectives, said he was sorry if he'd back-footed me and started off on some lecture about how little things in business, like your 'temper tantrum' as he called it, can bring clarity to the larger agendas, and then the bloody rude bastard cut me off to take another call. The non-execs and I have just finished meeting. We discussed the idea of trying to lure you back but the majority felt too much damage had already been done and voted down the idea."

There was a long silence on the tape.

"The press release just went out citing insurmountable differences in management philosophy as the reason the deal fell apart. It also includes a brief statement about your leaving the company. It's as neutral as we could make it, but I'm sure there will be much speculation about it in the days ahead. Now, it's all about damage control. Please understand that none of this is what I wanted but Beecroft and some of our Directors have made a Horlicks of all this. I'd like to help you in any way I can. Please call when you get this."

His mind was spinning. Under no circumstances would he have rejoined IPP. *Somehow it would never have been the same, but couldn't they at least have asked? As a courtesy?* He knew the answer, *but still . . .*

He replayed Chris' message to make sure he hadn't misheard

anything. Listening to it the second time felt like listening to the news on the radio, like it was a report about some other company, about some other CEO, and he began to quiet himself. *What do you care what they do now? That's their business, not yours. Move on, old son. Move on.*

He played the next message. "Buddy, where are you? I've got so much I want to tell you. Call me at home. I'll be in all night. I'm sorry about all this and I'm worried sick about you. Please, don't be a pig-headed redneck. Talk to me. Please?"

"Talk to me, my ass," he growled at the answering machine. "You're the last person on the face of the earth I'd talk to."

The final message was from David Dolan again asking Bud to call him, at the office or at home, any time he could. "I need to talk with you. Right away. *Right* away."

Bud reached him at his office and David began by telling him he was sorry that things had worked out for him the way they had.

"Goddamn, David, word sure does travel fast. How in the world do you know all this?"

"I got a call from Richard and then I got a call from a woman at GilbertBeard."

Bud started to ask about Richard's call until he heard David refer to a woman at GilbertBeard. "JJ Jennings?" he said.

"That's the one."

"What the hell did she want with you?"

"She called to tell me you'd lost your job. She thought I should know."

"So she put you up to this?"

"No, she didn't put me up to anything. I first called you because Richard called me—and that's a story in itself—and then I called because I wanted you to know that I'm sorry, that I'm here to help."

"What did she tell you?"

"She told me the whole long, ugly story. Said she was only doing her job. She sounded very upset and wants to talk with you."

"To say what?" Bud asked. "Listen, she went behind my back and I thought she was made of better stuff than that. The Board's decision was just business, but hers . . . well, I think what she did went beyond business."

"Did changing your mind about our deal go beyond business?" David asked. "You didn't really have any choice but to do what you did. And I think the same goes for her. I'm learning that even good folks get compromised on occasion by this meat grinder we call the corporate world. So, think about hearing her out. She says she only wants to set the record straight."

"What does she care now? I'm no longer her client. In case y'all have forgotten, I got my ass fired today."

"I don't think she cares if you're her client or not. I know you don't want to hear this, but I think she's in love with you."

"Come on, David, how many times do I have to tell you: debutantes don't hanker for boys from Hope Hull."

"I think this one does."

Bud was silent for a moment. "She's got a damn strange way of showing it."

"At times, don't we all?" David said.

Bud put his hand over the phone and cleared his throat. "What did old Dr. Mickey Mouse want?"

"Are you sitting down?"

"I happen to be."

"He called this morning to say his deal with you had fallen through and to see if he could do a deal with us."

"You're pulling my leg."

"I'm afraid not."

"Well I'll be!" Bud said. "That's what he'll do next. What'd you tell him?"

"He wanted to meet tonight, here in Princeton. I told him I would, but only to see what he has to offer. I hope that's okay with you."

"It's fine with me. I don't have any say in the matter, but thanks just the same."

"Thanks," David said. "He says he'll do anything it takes to see a deal with us go through."

Bud laughed. "I've heard that bullshit before. Verbatim."

"Well, he's bringing a formal proposal tonight, so we'll see. I think I'd be delinquent if I didn't talk with him but I don't dare tell Dad."

"There's no harm in hearing him out, David. Your dad should understand."

"I hope you're right. By the way, I got talking about Richard's visit with your . . . with JJ . . . and just before she hung up, she said I might be able to sell a minority interest in our business and make everybody happy."

"She's smart as a whip. I'll give her that," Bud said. "It sure as hell is something worth thinking on."

"Agreed. Now look, you've got a lot of friends in this business, and I'm at the head of the list, so if there's anything I can do to help—"

"I'm afraid *used to have friends* is the operative phrase," Bud blurted out. "I'm not much good to anybody anymore. All of a sudden I'm a nobody, but thanks anyway, and good luck tonight with Dr. Mickey Mouse. And you be careful, you hear?"

"Will do," David said. "And will you do me a favor and call that JJ woman?"

Bud said he'd give it another think. "But if I don't call her, don't take it personally. It'll be nothing more than another business decision."

David laughed. "I guess it all depends on where you draw the line. Just remember how hurtful some business decisions can be."

"Roger that," Bud said. "I hear you, loud and clear," and once again wished David luck with Beecroft and told him to keep his guard up. He set the phone gently on its cradle, stared out his bedroom window at the brightly lit houses across the street and felt very much alone, very much an outsider to all he had known for the past twenty-five years. He looked back down at the phone and muttered, "And please don't take it personally, old friend, but I think I'll stick to my guns. As difficult as that may be."

CHAPTER 18

With his hands clasped behind his back, his right eye covered by a gauze bandage, Richard paced across his office, his long legs carrying him from his desk to the window and back in no more than a handful of strides. "What have I forgotten?"

His secretary, a heavy woman with straight white hair and a raspberry-colored birthmark that spread across the upper left side of her face—hand-picked by Fiona as her replacement so that "Richard wouldn't be tempted to stray again"—flipped the pages of her stenography book with short, thick fingers. "Your meetings tomorrow all canceled . . . a call in to Secretary Benson . . . the proposal for Mr. Dolan . . . a room at The Four Seasons . . . your overnight kit ready to go." She looked up at Richard as he stopped at his desk. "All appears to be in order. All but one last thing: a call to Fi—" She caught herself and looked down at her notes. "You need to call your wife."

Richard looked at his watch. "Please call her for me. I'm late as it is. Give her my itinerary and extend my apologies. I'm sure she'll understand how important this trip is."

"Of course she will. She understands the pressure you're under better than anyone."

"And give Peter Benson one last go while I tidy up here."

"Of course, Dr. Beecroft." She uncrossed her doughy, blue-stockinged calves and pushed herself from the chair. "If I can't reach him, would you like me to leave a message?"

"Tell him I'm off to America to help him and the Prime Minister keep British pharma on British soil." He began sorting his papers, piling some on a corner of his desk, the others in his briefcase. Without looking up, he said, "Leave him my mobile number and ask him to call as soon as he can." When his secretary had closed the door to his office, Richard added, "That should please the bastards. No one can say I haven't upheld my end of our bargain. Now what about them?"

Moments later Richard stopped in front of his secretary's desk. She glanced up at him and pushed her glasses to the top of her head. "Secretary Benson has gone for the day. I left your message and asked him to call on your mobile. Will you have time to call your wife from the car or do you want me to ring her?"

"Margaret, I thought we agreed you'd call her," he snapped. "I've got more pressing matters at the moment."

"Of course. Have a safe journey and good luck with Mr. Dolan. All will be fine here, Dr. Beecroft. Not to worry. All is in good hands."

He began to salute good-bye but stopped as his index finger brushed the bandage over his eye. "Damn," he said and hurried to the garage where his driver was waiting for him.

Richard boarded the Concorde at twenty of seven and by six
o'clock New York time was seated in the back of a Lincoln
Town Car on his way to the Nassau Inn in Princeton. When
he arrived, David was waiting to greet him. "What in God's
name happened?" David asked. "And don't tell me I should see
the other guy."

"There was no other guy," Richard said, avoiding David's
eyes. "I tripped on the stairs outside my office." He looked
around the inn. "Do you have a table where we can talk?"

When David heard the imperious tone in Richard's voice
and felt his limp handshake he wondered if he'd made a mistake in agreeing to meet with him, no matter how speculative
their get-together was. He gestured toward the back of the
inn, and led Richard to a high-backed, wooden booth. "This
okay?"

"It will do." Richard folded his long frame onto a cush-
ioned seat, laid his briefcase beside him and opened it. He
started to hand David an envelope but paused as a waitress
asked if they would like to order a drink. He nodded at David
who ordered a Chivas Regal on the rocks. "I'll have the same,
neat," Richard said. "Do you understand? Just scotch in a glass.
No water. No ice."

The waitress raised her eyebrows at David. "I understand."

"Down to business?" David said.

Richard handed him the envelope. "I've brought our proposal in the form of a letter. It's a firm offer, and quite a gener-
ous one at that."

David nodded and opened the envelope. He stretched his
right leg and rubbed his hip and thigh vigorously for a few seconds, and then began to read.

Dear David:

*Following my phone conversation with you today, I am writing to
confirm my Company's strong desire to acquire Dolan Laboratories.*

We understand that recently the Dolan shareholders favorably considered a conditional all cash proposal for their company. Accordingly, subject to our own Board's final approval, Whitecliff Laboratories would like to make a similar cash offer for your company of US $4.0 billion. Our proposal is conditional on limited due diligence and would involve certain regulatory issues, but we are advised that these could be accommodated without undue difficulty.

We believe that your family is in a good position to appreciate the substantial benefits that would result from a combination between Dolan Laboratories and Whitecliff Laboratories . . .

He placed the letter on the table and smoothed it with his hand as the waitress set their drinks in front of them.

Richard raised his glass. "Cheers."

David nodded once but failed to lift his glass. "What happened to the 'substantial premium' you suggested on the phone?"

"Well, there was no way we could know what IPP offered so we assumed—"

"If you didn't know what IPP offered, how could you suggest a premium, let alone a *substantial* premium?"

"No matter," Richard said. "Four billion dollars is a lot of money, especially to one small family." He smiled. "Wasn't it one of your own who said if you make a billion here and a billion there, pretty soon it adds up to real money?"

David gripped the edge of the table with both hands. "A couple of things, Richard." He paused to center himself. "First, when you promised me a substantial premium, I took you for your word and assumed you'd meet your commitment. If you didn't know what IPP offered, as I suspect you did, you never should have brought a premium into the discussion. It's as simple as that. And, second—"

"Very well," Richard said. "What will it take for us to buy your company? Four point two. Four point two-five?"

"You're headed in the right direction but, as I was saying before you interrupted me, my second point was that, because of our history with you and Whitecliff, I was reluctant to even consider an offer from you, let alone meet with you. I only decided to hear you out to make sure I wasn't passing up an exceptional opportunity for my family. In turn, you had to know it was an uphill battle from the start." David didn't give him time to respond. "You also had to know that your lowball offer would be viewed as an insult; as another slap in my family's face. Is that what you intended?"

"This is not about insults," Richard said. "It's a negotiable offer for your family's business. A starting point."

"And an end point," David said. "I'm afraid, Richard, Dolan Laboratories is not for sale—certainly not to bottom feeders like you. I'm sorry you had to come all this way to find that out, but it was your idea to meet, not mine."

"Not for sale for any price?" Richard shook his head. "We all have our price, David, and I'm prepared to offer an additional two hundred and fifty million dollars as an act of good faith."

David sat quietly for a moment and rubbed his thigh. "I'm not sure how my family would react to that."

"Really? At four billion they were prepared to sell. Why wouldn't they jump at my offer?"

"Because you haven't *made* such an offer." He raised his hand and caught their waitress's eye. "Check, please?"

"Didn't I make myself clear?" Richard said. "I'll have it in writing to you tomorrow. Do we have a deal?"

"No, but here's what I'm prepared to consider. I'll sell you forty percent of our company for 1.7 billion dollars. You get co-marketing rights to all our drugs, including lomaxidine, and you have first rights of refusal to acquire more or all of us down the road."

"Your family would approve?"

David stared at Richard's good eye and said with all the authority he could muster, "Absolutely."

"Well," Richard said. "Excellent." He eased himself from the booth. "I think we're headed in the right direction. I'll have a letter of understanding drawn up tomorrow." He held out a limp hand and walked away.

David remained seated and took small, deliberate sips of his scotch while staring at the two rows of black and white photographs on the wall opposite him. They were of Princeton's most distinguished graduates, and all the names and many of the faces were familiar to him: John Foster Dulles, Class of 1908; Adlai Stevenson, '22; Archibald Dolan, '40; Bill Bradley, '65; Brooke Shields, '87. He stood to leave, walked closer to the pictures and studied the photograph of his father. *I wonder what he'll think of tonight's performance. I've struck a very good deal for his company, or is it my company?* He shrugged. *I'll know soon enough.*

CHAPTER 19

Fiona eased out of the Jacuzzi that Richard and she had installed—to "unwind in, among other things," she had joked—and reached for a thick, peach-colored towel. This was *her* morning, for Richard was in America, *trying to do another deal, trying to save his political ass,* she thought, *and didn't even have the common courtesy to call and tell me he was going.* But now the day, and the house, were hers. She was aware that when she felt in charge she experienced a feeling of euphoria, and her confidence—and her ability to see things clearly—improved greatly.

She dried herself and stepped in front of her full-length mirror and let her towel slide slowly to the floor. Her skin was pink from the warmth of her bath. She turned away and looked over her shoulder at the backs of her thighs. *No cellulite yet.* She moved in profile and smoothed her hands under her buttocks, flexed the well-rounded muscles, then gently lifted them and let them fall. She thought her butt was still firm and her calves and thighs still had a pleasing curve. *Things haven't changed all that much, if at all.* She traced the profile of her belly with her index finger, circled her finger through her blonde pubic hair and stood straight, dropping her arms at attention, studying her breasts to see if age had changed their posture. *Not bad for thirty-seven. Maybe as good as ever.*

She ran her hands over her rib cage, cupped them under her breasts and lifted them as if she were offering them to her image in the mirror. She stroked her nipples with her thumbs, watched them stiffen and felt her face warm. *Not many men can resist that. Certainly not Richard. It gets him hard in an instant.* But, now, she was convinced that Richard had married her for that, and that alone. *He cares a bloody lot more about his deals and feathering his own nest than he does about me. Well, he's not the only man in London who wants what I've got.* She stooped and picked up the towel, wrapped herself in it once again, and smiled. *Who's got what I want.*

Mid-morning she collected her house keys from the front hall table and dropped them in her purse and fastened her Barbour jacket, zipping it to its collar. She pulled an olive Stetson with a gold and brown pheasant feather band well down on her wavy blonde hair and slipped on a pair of dark glasses. Once outside she found the cold December air invigorating, even comforting, for it reminded her of winters in St. Helen's, her childhood home far north of London, where Lords and Ladies and megadeals were only something one read about in the newspapers. *Where you worked hard for everything you got—and even harder for what you really wanted, and didn't quit until you got it.*

She walked briskly toward Sloane Square, avoiding eye contact with all passers-by. At the edge of the square she stopped at the newsstand, reached into her purse for a ten-pound note and quickly listed the papers she wanted to buy: "*The Times, The FT, The Guardian* and *The Telegraph*." Almost as an afterthought, she said, "And . . . and . . . *The Galaxy*."

She took the papers without looking at them, folded them closed, and waited for the newsman to count her change. He handed it to her and said, "Don't I know you from somewhere, love?"

"I doubt it."

He looked her up and down. "In the tabloids, perhaps?"

She put her change in her purse and clasped it shut. "No . . . no," she stammered, and hurried into the crowd of faceless people and to a small restaurant at the far side of the square where she asked for a table away from the windows and waited for her tea to be served before spreading open the papers.

POP GOES THE MERGER BUBBLE! Clash of corporate egos and outbursts of higher childishness scuttle Whitecliff-IPP deal; Industry Sources Stunned— Haney steps down stretched across the front page of *The Financial Times.*

Corporate egos and higher childishness! If only they knew how right they got it! She slid *The FT* underneath the pile of papers and, as she had been trained to do as the once dutiful secretary to Whitecliff's Chairman, immediately turned to *The Daily Telegraph's* "City Comment." She thought if all this had taken place when she had been Richard's secretary, she would have simply told him how brilliant he was, taken his shorthand, set up his meetings, arranged his travel, and supported him at every turn. She would have accepted it all without a thought, all with a smile and spread her legs for him at every opportunity. All without as much as a whisper in the press. *But as his wife? As her own woman?*

She read the "City Comment" column carefully: *"Those close to Whitecliff and IPP say that Richard Beecroft and the American Bud Haney—two overpaid fat cats in many people's minds—while charged with maximizing the value of their respective companies, simply couldn't get their big wallets and bigger egos out of the way to figure out how to make the deal work. While IPP's Board ostensibly tried to salvage the merger, not so with Whitecliff. Institutional investors are already calling for Beecroft's head, and one must assume that almost all investors, if not all, will jump on this bandwagon soon."*

They're calling for Richard's head? As well they should! She closed *The Telegraph.* Beneath it, glaring up at her was *The Galaxy.* **TIT FOR TAT—WHITECLIFF'S BEECROFT JILTED BY IPP.** As violated as she felt by the headline, she was drawn to the text: *"Richard Beecroft, Chairman and Chief Executive of Whitecliff Laboratories, is getting a taste of his own prescription medicine. After breaking up the Anglo-American marriage of IPP and America's Dolan Laboratories two weeks ago, yesterday he was left at the altar by his newly found partner, IPP. While both sides claim that cultural and managerial differences led to the deal's downfall, those close to the situation say that Beecroft's last-moment demands scuttled the corporate marriage. Beecroft, who broke up his own marriage for his secretary, Page Three Girl Fiona Hart, was unavailable for comment."*

She combed *The Galaxy's* pages to see if they included a picture of her. Relieved that they didn't, she looked around her as casually as she could, and then slipped the paper to the bottom of her pile, knowing full well that all this had put an end to becoming Lady Beecroft.

She glanced at the headlines of *The Guardian* and *The Times* and thought there was nothing in either to fret about. She stood and placed the newspapers on the empty chair opposite her to clear a space on the small table and then sat, poured a second cup of tea, and crossed her arms hard across her ribs. She took a deep breath and fished a small box of pink stationery and a pen from her purse and tried to focus on what she planned to do next.

CHAPTER 20

"Dr. Beecroft?" the woman said softly. "Would you care for something to drink?"

Richard opened his eyes and glanced at the flight attendant, her square face and straight gray hair close to his. "A bottle of mineral water, and no further disturbances," he said, and turned his bandaged face toward the Concorde's small window. He could see a slight bow in the horizon and was amused by how clear things became at such a great speed, at such a great altitude. Not only could he see the curvature of the earth's surface, he could finally see his situation clearly and relaxed for the first time in almost three weeks for he was on his way home having pulled off a sound deal; having done all that had been asked of him. *Benson calls on a Sunday—"the best day of a dirty weekend" Fiona calls it—and I did what I was asked. How can I be faulted for that? Did what I was asked and more. And the end strategy with Dolan is brilliant. Britain won't lose a company to the Americans and I've strengthened Whitecliff immeasurably. Absolutely brilliant. The little tap on my shoulder is sure to follow. And her? She'll forgive me; even thank me for rescuing her from her common life to be-come Lady Beecroft.* He smiled. *Things are very much in hand. Very much in hand, indeed.*

Richard's driver met him outside customs. As usual, he was standing well behind the rows of other chauffeurs who held their placards announcing whom they were waiting for. And, as usual, Richard asked if he'd brought his mail. "I'm afraid there's enough to keep you busy for quite awhile, Dr. Beecroft," his driver said. In the car park Richard waited impatiently for him to unlock the Jaguar and open his door, anxious to get down to the business at hand. Once settled in the car, he noted that all was in routine order: neatly piled on the right rear seat was a small collection of newspapers; a large white envelope, bulging with mail, sat on top of them; and his mobile phone had been placed precisely on the center of the envelope.

He slipped the phone into the breast pocket of his suit jacket and pulled his mail toward him. As he began to unwind the string that fastened the heavy envelope, he glanced at the headline of *The Times:* **WHITECLIFF MERGER FAILS. Insurmountable cultural differences given as rationale. Haney squeezed out.** He tapped the phrase **Haney squeezed out** with his finger and smiled. "Brilliant," he mumbled, "I finally got the bastard." A sense of satisfaction came over him. It had been a struggle, but now all was in order. He noticed that his driver was watching him in the rear-view mirror, and waved at him, half to signal that he wasn't talking to him, half to dismiss him.

He rested the unopened envelope in his lap, watched his driver merge the sedan onto the A4, flicked on the light above him and lifted *The Times* exposing the salmon-colored *Financial Times* beneath it. He shook his head as though he were shaking water from his ears. *Corporate egos and outbursts of higher childishness! They never get the whole picture, but they got Haney, too.*

Other than the egos and childishness rubbish, it's almost too good to be true—and I can manage childishness, and I can manage stunned industry sources, especially when I stun them a second time with a successful bid for Dolan.

He dropped *The Times* and *The FT* on the floor of the car, exposing *The Galaxy's* **TIT FOR TAT**. He sucked in a deep breath and let it out. He took another and exhaled it noisily. He saw his driver check him in the mirror and forced a smile, and then searched the text of *The Galaxy's* story for a reference to Fiona's picture. When he found none, he felt himself calm. *Not too damaging,* he thought. *And I'll be ready to set the ledger straight soon enough, perhaps even win the day with the Dolan deal. All in all, neutral. Without that horrid picture—maybe even on the positive side.*

"Dr. Beecroft, permit me to interrupt for a moment," his driver said, "but the traffic is bloody awful headed into London tonight. I'd try the back roads but my traffic finder indicates they're at a snail's pace as well."

"Do what you must," Richard said. He gave a quick smile and pulled the last of the papers, *The Daily Telegraph,* toward him, and flipped to its "City Comment." He read it slowly, registering the comments that he knew he would have to address. *Calling for my head?* He told himself to think it through, to relax. He closed his good eye for a moment to black out the thoughts that swirled about him and then slipped the papers beneath the others on the car floor, burying *The Galaxy's* glaring **TIT FOR TAT** on the bottom of the pile. *All manageable,* he thought, and pulled the contents of the envelope free. On top of the thick stack of correspondence was a note from his secretary:

Dr. Beecroft—

Secretary Benson returned my call and I asked him to leave a message on your mobile. Also, Mrs. Beecroft left this envelope at the office late today and asked that I include it with your company mail. She said to be sure that you get it as soon as you get off the plane. Your first appointment Monday is at 9:00 with Communications. They want to set up a series of press interviews for you. I've marked all in your diary.

Have a nice weekend. See you Monday first thing.

Margaret.

He studied the pale pink envelope with "Richard" written on it in Fiona's delicate, cursive handwriting. He slapped the envelope against his knee, then dropped it on the papers in his lap and slid his phone from his jacket pocket. The first message was from his country neighbor James Beery, saying he would like a word with him over the weekend about a number of European Union regulations he thought Richard should be aware of. He asked if he would call him at his number in Over Wallop.

The second message was from Peter Benson. Richard pressed the phone against his ear to get every word. "Sorry I've been so hard to reach but I've been on the go a bit this week. I understand you have too, but with little success. The Prime Minister and I have talked about your comings and goings, and while he's quite pleased that it looks as though IPP may remain a British company, he was very disappointed with the way it happened—the way *you* handled it—and about the press coverage you and your wife received. So, I'm afraid, at the end of the day, that little tap on the shoulder has been taken off the table. Sorry to have to deliver this type of news this way, but I guess it's the new way of doing things. You know, voice mail and all. Cheers for now."

Richard felt his chest tighten, his breathing become labored. He put his free hand to his mouth as he felt bile build in his throat. Clumsily he punched **1** to listen to his messages again, skipping over James Beery's to re-hear Peter Benson. *Perhaps I didn't hear him properly.* He wiped sweat from his temples and above his ears. "The Prime Minister . . . very disappointed

. . . the way *you* handled it and about the press coverage you and your wife received . . . that little tap on the shoulder has been taken off the table . . ."

Oh, my God, doesn't he know I was doing it all for him? Unfair! Just because my wife was a tart? She posed for those pictures, not me. Why must I bear her burden too?

His heartbeat was rapid and powerful. He ripped the bandage from his eye, crumpled it in a ball and threw it at his feet. He covered his heart with his hand to quiet it but quickly pulled his hand from his chest. His shirt was soaked through and growing cold. He dropped the phone on the floor of the car, grabbed both knees tightly, and shook his head back and forth.

"Is everything all right, Dr. Beecroft?" his driver asked.

"Of course," he whispered.

"Very good, sir. We should be at Alexander Terrace in another ten, fifteen minutes at most."

Richard lifted his hands and held them open in front of him, briefly studied their tremors, then clenched them into fists. He leaned forward and began beating them on his knees when he noticed the letter from Fiona. He ran a finger hard under the envelope seal and pulled the note free. He held it with both hands barely six inches from his eyes, struggling to steady the paper, straining to read Fiona's handwriting with his one good eye, handwriting that he had known so well from her as his secretary but could never remember reading from her as his wife.

Dear Richard,

When you read this letter, I will have left you and gone home to St. Helen's to be with my parents and with people who truly love me; to be with my friends who remember me for who I am, not as page three girl Fiona Hart, and who realize that posing for that picture was a horrible, childish mistake, but who also understand that people struggling as I was do what they have to do to get by—something you never really understood. In a funny way I think you should understand better than most, for men in your position live by the same rules as I did, Richard. You all just disguise them better.

As a result of the events of the last three weeks, I've learned so much about you and me—and myself. One thing that I should have realized long ago as your secretary is now so obvious to me—business and ambition for Richard Beecroft come first. All else, including me, is secondary. I can't stand how that makes me feel, nor can I stand the humiliation you've brought upon me, and upon us.

I'm sure the unfortunate way things have turned out is as much my fault as it is yours, but as you've often told me, when things aren't going well, it's best to cut your losses and move on. So, you see, Richard, you're still the boss and, as I so often have in the past, once again I'm taking your advice.

Please know that I believe our marrying was a mistake for <u>both</u> of us. I thought I wanted to be Lady Beecroft so badly, but now know that would have been nothing but a charade. And I've come to realize that my happiest times with you were when we worked together, when I wasn't in the limelight, even though being married to Sir Richard Beecroft was something I always thought sounded so wonderful.

I hope the world treats you fairly with all the things you're trying to do.

I'm rambling a bit, I know, but this is a very difficult letter for me to write, and an even more difficult decision for me to make. It's odd, considering all the important letters that I drafted for you over the years, that I can't think how to close this one, except to say, please don't try to reach me.

I'm sorry, Richard, for both of us, but especially for me, for it all seemed to be in your hands. I'll call you when I feel strong enough to talk about where we head next.

Fiona

He stared at the letter, turned it over to see if more was written on the back of the page. His heart raced. He found it difficult to breathe. His body was covered in sweat. Again a foul taste crept up his throat to the back of his mouth.

The silver sedan pulled close to the curb, beneath the street-light on Alexander Terrace. Richard's driver reached for his hat and pulled it on as he climbed from the car. He walked quickly to the rear door and opened it. The overhead light flooded the back seat where Richard lay curled in the fetal position, his hands jammed between his knees.

"My God, sir, are you all right?" his driver asked.

Richard raised his head. His right eye was swollen shut, a bulging blending of purple, red and green. His left eye had the look of a dog struck by a car, begging for help. He shook his head slightly, pushed his hands further between his legs and continued to plead with his one good eye. "I need help. Please, help me," he murmured. "I must find a way to explain that I did all that was asked of me, and more. So much more."

CHAPTER 21

David settled in behind his large desk, swiveled his chair aimlessly and stared at the thick signature file sitting in front of him. There were times when he imagined that his desk shielded him from the rest of the world; acted as a fortress from which to deal with the pressures of managing his family's business, and this was one of those times. He pushed the file to one side and reached for the phone, dialed and waited for an answer. "I hope I didn't wake you," he said.

"I've been up for hours," his father said. "I can't seem to sleep much since your mother died."

"I know. I dream about her all the time, but they're really nice dreams and she looks so young, so healthy." He paused and waited for his father to respond. "Well, if you're not too busy, I'd like it if you'd drop by the office this morning. I've got some things I'd like to talk about with you."

Arch didn't answer right away. "What's wrong with coming out to Fox Hill?"

"I think it would be better to talk here, " David said. "I've got some company issues I'd like to discuss."

Again, Arch hesitated. "Have it your way. I'll be there in an hour or so."

While waiting for his father to arrive, David went through his signature file. The last papers in the file were three copies of a letter of intent between Dolan and Whitecliff Laboratories. He read the letter carefully and then closed the folder and placed all the copies on top of it. He pushed his chair from his desk, massaged his right thigh and gazed out the window at the winding drive of the Dolan Research Campus. He wondered if he should show the letter to his father before signing it. As he weighed his decision, a black Ford Taurus station wagon came into sight. He stared at the car for a moment, swiveled his chair and pulled himself close to his desk. Again, he looked out the window and watched his father get out of his car and face the building, his large hands stuffed in the pockets of a heavy green loden coat. *I wonder what he's thinking. This is his building? The house he built? His name's over the door? His father's name's over the door?*

David watched him walk toward the entrance to the building where he was greeted with a salute from one of the security staff. In the frigid winter air each man's breath steamed from his mouth as he spoke. He wondered what his father was saying to him. *My son's selling out on me? Wouldn't stand and fight?* He turned again and ran the tip of his pen from top to bottom above the document in front of him. When he reached the line that read *s/for Dolan Laboratories,* he quickly scrawled his name and the date, then signed the second copy and then the third.

"There," he said aloud. He neatened the papers and placed them back in the folder. "I've done it." *Dad's almost seven hundred million dollars richer and Uncle Ben and Aunt Sarah three hundred million each.* A feeling of relief, calm and confidence came over him. He smiled. "Why, what the hell, I've made them rich as Croesus." He knew that was exactly what his father would have said, but today, for some reason, it didn't matter.

Arch removed his coat, draped it over one of the chairs that faced his son's desk and lowered himself into the other. "What's happened now?"

What have you done this time? David thought. "Nothing's happened." *Or maybe everything's happened.* "I've been thinking that the best possible deal for us would be to sell a minority interest in our company and merge our product line with our new partner's. That way we'd remain independent *and* profitable."

"That's what you're recommending?"

David reached for the folder and pulled one of the copies of the letter of intent from it. He leaned across his desk and handed the letter to his father. "It's all here. All the terms in summary. It'll only take a minute to read."

Arch took the letter and read it slowly. He gave David a puzzled look. "Why . . . why, you've signed this. This is a done deal."

"Right," David said. "And a good one at that."

Arch flipped the letter onto David's desk. "You signed it without even discussing it with me. What's more, if I'd been you, I'd have never, ever—even if he was the last man on earth—done business with that self-centered son of a bitch Beecroft. I'll never forgive him for what he tried to do to our company, to our family name."

"Well, maybe times and circumstances have changed," David said. "Maybe Richard has, too. Forgive and forget. Isn't that what we're all trying to do?"

Arch gave him a confused look and shook his head.

"Does that mean you'll vote Mom's and your shares against it?"

Arch remained silent and closed his eyes for a moment. When he opened them, they were bright with tears, tears the old man didn't try to hide. "That's what your mother and I were talking about the morning she died. She said I'd had my turn; that I had to let go. She asked me to support you and I promised I would. So, from here on out, I'm just another family member who will do anything you ask of me, but if it were up to me, I wouldn't lift a finger to help that man—but there I go doing just what I promised I wouldn't do." He pushed himself from his chair, pulled on his coat and struggled with the wooden handle-like buttons as he slipped each through its loop. He leaned forward and tapped the agreement with his large-knuckled index finger. "That's the best you could do?"

"I think it's the best anyone could do, given the circumstances. We're in a very difficult spot and this will see us through it. Who knows, someday we may even be able to buy back Whitecliff's share."

Arch stared at his son for a moment. "That would be nice," he said, and turned to leave.

"Before you go, Dad, I've got to ask you a question. How come you never told me you offered the presidency to Bud?"

Arch raised his bushy white eyebrows and craned his neck forward. "Who told you that?"

"Bud did."

"Well, I didn't offer it to him; I only discussed it in principle."

"But what would you have done if he'd accepted?"

"It never got that far. The minute I raised it with him, he said he wouldn't even consider it."

"But what if he had? Why didn't you come to me first and ask me what I thought was best? What *I* wanted?"

"Look, son, it was a mistake. A huge mistake. I hadn't

thought it all the way through and, to be honest with you, I don't know what I would have done if he had shown interest. At the time I thought I was doing what was best for our company—you know, exploring all my options. Your mother was furious with me. She said I'd handled it horrendously and said you'd make a fine chief executive."

"You know, if you'd asked me back then what I wanted, I might have told you to give him the job, that I'd rather do something else," David said. "But now . . . now I'll never let go. There's too damn much of me invested in this business."

Arch stared down at him. "I'm glad to hear you say that. Your mother would be delighted, too." He reached his hand across the desk. David took it and stood. "I think you're right," his father said. "Given the circumstances, your deal with Whitecliff is the best anyone could do."

David smiled. "Thank you, sir."

Arch nodded. "Will I see you tomorrow for lunch?"

"We're planning on it if you still are. The girls are coming, too."

Arch smiled. "Good. Same time, same station."

David watched his father hobble stiffly from his office and disappear down the hallway. He walked to the window and, out of habit, massaged his thigh. He wondered if it all had been worth it. His wish to be in charge, to be on his own, had finally been granted but he never thought the moment would come with so much pain and alienation. And he wondered if he'd made the right decision to stay with the family business, especially when he sensed he was at the helm by default. Wondered if he should have chosen to do what his father had so desperately opposed? If he'd done the right thing by cutting a deal—no matter how good a deal it was—with Richard Beecroft, a man he didn't like, let alone didn't trust.

Endless questions, he thought, *all the answers a matter of judgment. No rights. No wrongs. Just endless judgments. Only time will tell.*

Below him, leaves left behind from the fall's last raking stirred with the cold December wind and flitted across the manicured lawn of his research campus, the research campus that will remain his, and his family's, as long as he was in charge. He watched his father unlock his car and look up at him and wave as though he knew he would be there. A small white cloud rose from his mouth.

Thank you? Did he say thank you? David raised his hands palms up and then cupped his ears to signal he didn't understand what his father had said, but the old man simply waved again and eased himself into his car. *Maybe I'll find out tomorrow. Maybe it's a beginning. Maybe it's not so bad being the last man standing.*

CHAPTER 22

Dark tea spilled from the china cup Richard carried as he paced across his kitchen, stepping over and around—and occasionally kicking at—the colorful piles of clothes strewn at his feet. He was partially dressed for church. He wore Wellington boots, olive corduroy trousers, and a green and blue tattersall shirt unbuttoned almost to his waist. His thinning dark hair stood in tufts about his head. He stopped at the sink and emptied his tea and looked through the small lead-framed window at his garden that was now bathed in the early morning sun. He turned his head in circles to relieve the tension in his neck and placed the cup on the side of the sink. He stepped back, stared at the cup for a moment, then moved it to the right no more than an inch and wiped his hands together in a satisfied manner.

He turned and studied the clothes on the floor and then took a carton of plastic trash bags from a drawer beneath the sink. He dropped to his hands and knees and in sweeping motions drew Fiona's clothes across the linoleum to him and stuffed them in the bags. He stopped at the pile of her underwear and inspected each item as he threw it in the bag—Wonder bras, camisoles, bikini underpants. He lifted her black lace thong panties, pressed them to his face and inhaled the fresh smell of laundry detergent, then tore them in half before forcing them to the bottom of a bag. When he had collected all of her clothes, he carried the bulging black bags outside and dropped them in the covered dustbin at the back of the cottage. Again, he wiped his hands together in a satisfied manner. *Good riddance to bad rubbish. Isn't that what they say?*

He took the water bucket from the dog kennel and walked inside the house. As he ran water into the bucket, he glanced at his watch. *People should be headed to Nether Wallop soon,* he thought. He filled an aluminum bowl with dog food, the sound of the kibble pouring into the bowl waking his yellow Labrador, who pushed up from his bed in the corner of the kitchen and followed Richard outside. He set the water bucket at the back of the kennel, placed the bowl of food beside it and watched as the dog began to eat. He raised a finger to the eyebrow above his bulging purple eyelid, gave his dog a casual salute and bolted the kennel door shut. "It's okay, Cider, the caretaker will be here first thing in the morning." The dog continued to take large, noisy mouthfuls. Richard shook his head. "You're no different than all the rest. You don't give a damn about what I have to say either."

Cider finished eating and looked up at his master. There was a playful look in his eyes as he began wagging his tail. Richard unlatched the kennel gate, took a few steps and knelt. He placed his hands on the dog's ears and massaged them and then lifted his muzzle so that his eyes were looking directly at him. "I did all they asked of me. I swear I did." He smoothed his hand over the crown of the dog's head, patted his shoulder and stood and took one last look at him. "Be a good boy, Cider. I'll miss you."

Once back inside the small cottage, Richard locked the doors and drew each and every window shade until the downstairs was almost completely dark. He walked back to the kitchen, flicked on the overhead light and stared at his teacup. He washed it, dried it and put it in the cabinet from which he had taken it and looked around the kitchen once more before switching off the light.

At the head of the narrow stairs to his bedroom, he ducked his head as he stepped through the low doorjamb. He took two large stainless keys from his bureau, opened his closet door, and unlocked a steel cabinet that was hidden behind his hanging clothes. A shotgun stood upright in the gray foam-padded interior. He took a folded copy of *The Galaxy* from the bottom of the cabinet, picked two dark green twenty gauge cartridges from a box marked *Holland & Holland,* lifted the shotgun and backed from the closet. With his free hand he straightened his clothes and shut the closet door and laid the gun and the cartridges on his bed.

He opened *The Galaxy* to page three, creased the paper and placed it on the pillow on the far side of the bed; the pillow Fiona used to lay her head on, the one at times she had hurriedly placed under her buttocks to get more of Richard and Richard more of her. He stared at Fiona's picture and then looked away. He drew a pen, a small pad of paper and an envelope from his nightstand and sat on the bed. He wrote for a moment, then stopped, sucked on the end of the pen and wrote some more, and then folded the paper and slipped it into the envelope.

His note read:

To all you vultures—and you know who you are.

Don't you, Fiona? Don't you, Peter Benson? And all you nameless, faceless cowards in the media.

Why did you do this to me? All I ever did was what was asked of *me. And what was my reward? Once again I'm the laughingstock—a failure in everything that is important to me. <u>That</u> is my reward. How could I have ever believed you, Benson, about my knighthood?*

How can I ever trust anyone going forward? There is nothing left for me to do.

And I didn't pose for that picture. You did, Fiona. Damn you woman, <u>you did!</u> And it all would have worked if only you hadn't. I've lost all hope of ever attaining the things that mean the most to me. How can I be faulted for that?

How can I? I don't understand. Fiona, how can you fault me so?

He cocked his head and listened for a moment. In the distance he could hear the bells as they began to ring at St. Andrew's. He wrote *For All You Vultures* on the envelope and placed it at the entrance to the room, facing the writing toward the stairs. He wiped his hands again as though he had completed another major task and lifted the shotgun. He ran his left hand the length of the cold, blue-black barrels and shouldered the gun as though he were shooting at a bird. He lowered it, wiped sweat from his temple and the back of his neck, opened the gun, inserted a cartridge in each barrel, and snapped it shut. He put the gun to his shoulder again and leaned across the bed and pressed the muzzle to the picture of Fiona's face, drawing it down beneath her neatly styled blonde hair, beneath her large blue eyes, onto her open mouth, to the tip of her tongue that was licking her upper lip. He thumbed the safety forward and pulled the trigger. The gun pushed against his shoulder, its report muffled by the pillow behind Fiona's picture.

Richard lowered the gun and studied the photograph. A charred-edged hole slightly larger than a pound coin replaced Fiona's suggestive mouth. "Good riddance to bad rubbish," he said. He looked out his window and for a moment watched a man and a woman walk along the lane toward his cottage. He pulled the shade. Everything was now in shadows and for a moment he felt secure.

He sat on the edge of the bed, struggled to pull off his Wellingtons, and set them, side by side, on the floor at the end of the bed. Once again he lifted the shotgun and lay down and tucked his knees to his chest. He rested the gun beside him and lifted his head to look at Fiona's picture. The light in the bedroom was now gray-black, with only a thin yellow sliver shining at the bottom of the shade, and he could barely make out Fiona's image on the printed page. He leaned across the gun's cold barrels and placed his lips against Fiona's gaping mouth and held them there. Finally, he lifted his head, straightened his body and lay back on his pillow. Tears ran down his cheeks. Their warmth comforted him. "You're not rubbish at all, my love," he whispered. "I didn't mean that. I'm in a bit of a muddle right now."

As James Beery and his wife neared the entrance to White Gate Cottage on their way to the ten-thirty service at St. Andrew's, they wondered if Richard and Fiona would make an appearance at church, or if the rumors that they had separated were true. Beery told his wife that he might learn some news about them soon, for he had a call in to Richard and expected to hear from him before the weekend was over. In the distance the bells at St. Andrew's continued to ring and neither James Beery, nor his wife, seemed to notice the muted thud that came from White Gate Cottage as they strolled past.

CHAPTER 23

Unaware of Richard Beecroft's death—that news would not reach the media for several days—Bud was standing on the small stoop outside his front door, pulling his keys from the pocket of his aviator's jacket when he heard a familiar voice.

"Buddy?"

He pretended not to hear and continued to grapple with his keys. He unlocked the top of two locks when the caller said, "Buddy, please. Talk to me."

He leaned forward and inserted the second key in the lower lock.

"Please."

He thought he couldn't remember JJ ever pleading with him and didn't think he could just go in his house and shut the door on her. He turned and looked down at her from the low, marble landing. She stood at the edge of the sidewalk, almost in the street, her long brown hair blowing across her face. The way her hands were pushed deep into the pockets of her cream-colored fleece jacket, he couldn't tell if she was warming herself or settling in for a fight.

She swept her hair behind her ears and looked up at him. "I tried to reach you all weekend. Please, what harm can talking do?"

"You and I've got nothing to talk about," he said.

"Maybe you don't, but I do. I want to explain what happened." He thought she was struggling to get her bearings, to find her "banker's face" somehow. "All I'm asking for is five minutes."

He folded his arms across his chest. "Five minutes, no more."

"Buddy, could you come down here and talk to me please?"

"Okay, but knock off that 'Buddy' nonsense."

JJ smiled. "Yes, sir, Mr. Haney."

He felt himself growing angry with her—or maybe with himself—because she was doing just what he didn't want her to do—trying to charm her way back into his good graces—and he felt himself weakening. He walked down the steps to the sidewalk and slipped his hands in the back pockets of his pants and stared at her. "What can you tell me that I don't already know?"

"I don't know. I just had to make sure you heard my side of it." She paused, appearing to wait for some form of acknowledgment, but Bud continued to stare at her without speaking. "When Chris asked me to come to that dinner, he said he wanted his Directors to hear the various scenarios and their impact on the share price from a third party because he felt Nigel might inject his personal bias. He kept saying he didn't want any editorializing on my part or on Nigel's either, for that matter."

He drew his hand from his pocket and looked at his watch. "I've still got some time left and I want you to pay attention here, Mr. Haney," JJ said. "This is important to me. The first thing I asked Chris was if you would be at the dinner, and when he said 'no' and I asked why not, he said he didn't want you threatened by all of it, that he thought it might dampen your effectiveness at the meeting the next day. He ended the call by telling me not to worry, that he was on your side and had no intention of doing business with a man like Richard Beecroft."

"Well, I'll be damned," Bud said. "Good old Sir Christopher."

"As always," JJ said. "Good old Sir Christopher. Good old, good old boys. But no good old JJ. Can't you see what an impossible position I was in? The only way I could have helped you would have been to lie to your Board, and you know I don't do that."

"But you could have told me what happened before I went into the Board meeting; before I ended up looking like a damn fool."

"Chris told me not to breathe a word and, don't forget, it's his show."

"But as a . . ." He stopped.

With her hands still deep in her pockets, JJ turned slightly from side to side. "As a what?"

"I don't know," he said quietly. "I guess you were doing your job, but, damn, JJ, it made me feel like you'd jumped ship on me."

"I know it did, and I'm sorrier than you'll ever know. For the first time in my life I hated doing my job. You've got to believe me."

"Okay, okay, but why'd you have to bring David Dolan into all of this?"

"I thought he should know what happened to you and I didn't think anyone else would call—"

"But you tried to get to me through him."

"Yes, I did. I was desperate. You wouldn't answer—"

"Hey, look: first you talked about me behind my back to

my Board, and then you went and called a man you'd never even met and talked to him about me. It made me feel like some kind of freak in a sideshow or something; like I didn't have any say in what was going on with my life."

"I was only trying to help. Don't you understand?"

At first he shook his head and then he said, "I guess I do."

"Well, we're getting there," JJ said. "Also, I called David to give him a thought I had about selling his company."

"You lay awake nights dreaming that stuff up?"

"It beats counting sheep," she said. "Besides, I don't have anything better to do."

Bud laughed. "Well, you just may have saved David's bacon." He waved his hand in the direction of the Thames. "Come on. Let's take a walk." They walked for a moment in silence before he asked, "What else you got?"

"What will happen with Chris Pearson and Nigel?"

"I guess right now they're scrambling to find another deal, but they'll survive. The Board won't let anything happen to them, not after my debacle. They've had their fill of instability." He shrugged. "Life at IPP will just keep on truckin' on."

"And Richard?"

"Who ever knows what Richard will do? My guess is he'll go underground for a while."

"And you? What will *you* do now?"

He shrugged and looked down at the pavement. "I don't have the slightest idea. I guess I'll be going back to the US soon to work all this out. Maybe I'll go back to Hope Hull for a while. Hell, I don't know much of anything right now. I don't really have a place I call home. IPP's become my whole identity and I'm not sure what I'll do without it. All I know is, it's time for me to find some roots."

"I know my five minutes are up—"

"Long ago."

"But I have one last question."

They turned down the Pimlico Road and walked toward the river.

"Fire away," he said.

"Are you badly hurt?"

He looked down at the sidewalk again. "I'm okay, I guess." And then he looked up. "Who the hell am I kidding? Hell, yes I'm hurt. I'm angry, too. I feel like things are closing in on me—like I'm a POW again. Keeping it all straight is like trying to stack a bunch of snakes. I'm confused. I'm angry. I'm claustrophobic. I'm hurt. I'm embarrassed. I'm a whole bunch of bad things right now."

Almost in a whisper JJ said, "I understand."

"Maybe you do and, then again, maybe you don't. I've been a loner all my life and I've never really known what I'm feeling, and this whole deal has only made things worse. Face it, JJ, I'm nothing more than a businessman. All I've ever done is solve problems, rely on facts, set objectives, all that cerebral stuff. That's all I know how to do. It hasn't been just all work and no play; it's been all think and no feel, too. The odd thing is, no matter how many times I go over it in my mind, I wouldn't change a thing I did with IPP, or Dolan, or Whitecliff for that matter, but for some reason, it all still confuses the hell out of me. Maybe it's as simple as I just don't like losing."

"Maybe, but maybe it's not because you're an executive. Maybe it's just you. Maybe you're afraid of knowing what you're feeling." She smiled at him. "I think I could help you with that."

He caught himself staring at her. "I wouldn't even know where, or how, to start," he said. "I think I gave up on all that type of stuff long ago." He stopped walking and looked at his watch.

"Time's up?" she said. "Just when things were getting interesting."

"It's almost one o'clock," he said. "You hungry?"

"Are you offering to take me to lunch, Mr. Haney?"

"Yes, ma'am, I am."

"Okay," she said. "On one condition: you buy."

"How come?" he asked.

"Because you're no longer my client, and I'm no longer your banker."

"What are you then?" He was startled by his question and waited while JJ measured her answer.

Finally she said, "This is boy meets girl stuff, Buddy, and I'm just a lonely girl in a foreign land who thinks she can help a boy she cares about get through a very tough time. Help him move on. Find a new life. Maybe even find some roots."

"That'll do for starters," he said, and began to walk again.

JJ took a few quick steps to catch up and hooked her arm through his. He admired her thin, delicate hand and, instinctively, pulled her arm to his side, then quickly released it. They took a few more strides, almost in lock step, and Bud looked directly at her. She was smiling. "Ah, what the hell," he said, and pinned her arm hard against him once again.

"Ah, what the hell," JJ said, and tightened her grip on him, taking his arm firmly in her hand.

AFTERWORD

True stories never really end; they just keep unfolding, changing direction, adding or deleting characters, and unfold some more. So why should this one be any different? But—as far as most industry observers were concerned—this story was wrapped up in two articles, the first in the Friday, March 3 *Financial Times:*

A danse macabre that stopped and started, twisted and turned for six months has reached its climax with only two of the three dancers left on the floor, Whitecliff Laboratories and America's family-owned Dolan Laboratories, while International Pharmaceutical Products, the company that initiated the round of dancing, has vanished from the scene.

In a brief statement, Robert Murphy, Whitecliff's newly appointed chairman and chief executive, announced that his company had acquired a 40% interest in Dolan Laboratories for £1.1bn, giving them worldwide marketing rights to Dolan's existing product line and future compounds. "We are quite excited about Dolan's new product pipeline, especially DL63037—now lomaxidine—their promising new drug for memory loss and Alzheimer's," Murphy said. "We feel that we have greatly strengthened our company's prospects for the future."

Analysts in The City and on Wall Street received the acquisition of lomaxidine, widely referred to as "Viagra for the brain," enthusiastically as well. Elizabeth Eva of Smith Barney called the deal brilliant: "With lomaxidine performing well in phase three clinical trials and the FDA indicating that they will fast track it for approval, Whitecliff has added another jewel to its crown."

Whitecliff's shares closed yesterday at a record high of 1671p. At the same time, IPP's share price tumbled to 635p, slightly lower than its pre-merger discussion levels with both Dolan and Whitecliff. Institutional shareholders are pressing IPP's chairman, Sir Christopher Pearson, and his new chief executive, Donald Hardison, to quickly do another deal to recoup their significant loss in market value—or resign.

On a related matter, yesterday IPP announced that Nigel Finch-Hatton, the company's CFO, would retire, effective immediately. Estimates drawn from the IPP Report and Accounts show that Mr. Finch-Hatton will collect approximately £7.3m in severance pay and stock options.

The second article ran the same day in The Daily Telegraph's "City Comment":

Turning to Whitecliff's acquisition of Dolan Laboratories and IPP's inability to close a deal with either company, many in The City have gone beyond their usual terse financial analysis to volunteer their views on the human toll taken during these on-again off-again negotiations. One analyst (who asked to remain anonymous) even went so far as to ask if it was all worth it. The answer most frequently heard in The City is a resounding "Yes," especially if you're a shareholder, even though the IPP/Dolan/Whitecliff transactions were marred by more publicly visible personal tragedy than most, with one man losing his marriage and then taking his own life, and another—one of London's most highly paid and highly regarded executives—witnessing a twenty-five year career go down in flames, not for his lack of performance but to satisfy shareholders' expectations.

We've known all along that those steering our largest corporations are a breed apart in the pressures they face and the salaries they earn, but the events that transpired in this circular round of acquisitiveness indicate that—perhaps—the gap between these executives and the man on the street may not be as great as we once thought.

Perhaps?

AUTHOR'S NOTE

Thanks to the following for their valuable contributions:

My mentors in the Master of Fine Arts in Writing program at Vermont College, with special thanks to Bret Lott, whose enthusiasm from the very first draft kept me writing, and those other patient souls who read the early manuscript with a critical eye: Anne Dubuisson Anderson, Chris Noël, Rachel Simon and Whitney Ellsworth.

The fabulous boys of Mojo Marketing—my son Harry, Walter Ife and Dimitri Scheblanov—who helped in ways too numerous to list to get this book into your hands.

My great friends Charlie Hatfield and Peter Strawbridge; Charlie for giving me an insider's view of Princeton and Peter for spending many a breakfast discussing the torturous final chapters to his family's business, a recounting that helped mold—along with professional advice from Dr. Edward Monte—David Dolan's struggles in these pages.

Bill Gast and Justin Moll at Mangos for their creation of The Connelly Press logo; Betty Kapeghian who made sure all the i's were dotted and the t's crossed; sage advisor on all printing matters, George Nichols; Clive Reynard who represented me so vigorously in the UK; and Deirdre Snyder, the photographer with the flattering eye.

And above all, my wife Lyn who has suffered the emotional rollercoaster ride of my writing experiences far more than she needed, all the while shining light into the murky corners of my mind.

ABOUT THE AUTHOR

Harry Groome began writing as a stringer for the *New York Herald Tribune* while in high school. After a business career of almost forty years during which he retired as Chairman of SmithKline Beecham Consumer HealthCare and served on corporate boards both in the United States and the United Kingdom, Harry returned to writing. His short stories have appeared in numerous journals and anthologies and have received several awards. *Wing Walking* is his first novel.

ABOUT THE TYPE

Wing Walking was set in Bembo. Based on a typeface cut by Francesco Griffo in 1495, Bembo was first used for the Italian Cardinal Pietro Bembo's short text, *De Aetna*. The typeface that we see today is a revival by Stanley Morison for the Monotype Corporation in London of that old-style Roman typeface and other typefaces that had been lost for centuries. Designed in 1929, The Lanston Monotype Company of Philadelphia brought Bembo to the United States in the 1930s. The well-proportioned letterforms are quiet and simple, providing unusual legibility and a timeless, classical character.